Here's what people are saying about *Step into the Bible*

"This book is a children's Christian classic. I am happy to recommend it to all parents, and urge them to take advantage of its unique approach. I know of no book on the market like it."

— **Billy Graham**

"I was raised on Foster's *First Steps for Little Feet.* When our five children were growing up, I found it an invaluable help. You can start with a three-year-old and take him gradually through the Scriptures. I urged my daughter, Ruth, to re-do and bring it up to date. She has done this beautifully—an undertaking I am sure Foster himself would approve and be grateful for."

— **Ruth Bell Graham**

"Ruth Graham has put together an absolutely wonderful book for families. The questions and Memory Verses are a perfect way to help your children learn to love God. When parents mentor their children, the legacy of faith continues from generation to generation."

— **Jim Burns, Ph.D.**
President, HomeWord
Author of *Confident Parenting*

"As a mom of five children, this book will be on the top of my list of tools to help me teach my children biblical principles in a relevant and applicable way. Thank you, Ruth, for updating this classic for families to use today. I give this book my highest recommendation."

— **Lysa TerKeurst**
President of Proverbs 31 Ministries, speaker and author

"How many times as parents have we longed for the luxury of raising our children in the gentle wisdom of 'the good old days.' *Step into the Bible* provides the heritage of timeless truths with delightful illustrations and photographs that captivate a child's attention and heart."

— **Lisa Whelchel**
Bestselling author of *Creative Correction, The Facts of Life and Other Lessons My Father Taught Me,* and *Taking Care of the "Me" in Mommy*

Step into the Bible

100 Bible Stories for Family Devotions

Ruth Graham

ZONDERVAN®

ZONDERVAN.com/
AUTHORTRACKER
follow your favorite authors

www.zondervan.com

Step into the Bible
Copyright © 2007 by Ruth Graham

Adaptation of *First Steps in the Bible* © 1980 by Ruth Graham Dienert

Requests for information should be addressed to:
Grand Rapids, Michigan 49530

Library of Congress Cataloging-in-Publication Data

Graham, Ruth, 1950-
    Step into the Bible : 100 Bible stories for family devotions / by Ruth Graham.
      p. cm.
    ISBN-13: 978-0-310-71410-1 (softcover)
    ISBN-10: 0-310-71410-9 (softcover)
    1. Bible stories, English. 2. Bible--Devotional literature. 3. Family--Religious life. I. Title
BS550.3.G73 2007

   220.9'505--dc22
                                      2007017909

Published in association with the literary agency of Ambassador Literary Agency, Nashville, TN 37205.

Editor: Kristen Tuinstra
Theological Review: Michael J. Klassen, M.Div., Fuller Theological Seminary
Art Direction and Cover Design: Kris Nelson
Interior Design: Studio Montage
Composition: Studio Montage and Matthew Van Zomeren

Printed in China

08 09 10 11 12 • 14 13 12 11 10 9 8 7 6 5 4

Contents

In loving memory of my mother, who taught me the Scriptures with
First Steps for Little Feet Along Gospel Paths by Charles Foster.

May the little people in your life learn about the
Bible in this revised and updated edition of Foster's original book.

~ R.G.

Todd Bauders/Contrast Photography

Introduction

Four Generations

Step into the Bible is based on the book *First Steps for Little Feet Along Gospel Paths* by Charles Foster. First published in the 1800s, this book taught the Bible to four generations of Graham children. It has stood the test of time with updates and re-releases over the past 150-plus years.

Many years ago, when my grandparents were medical missionaries to China, they chose *First Steps for Little Feet Along Gospel Paths* to teach their children biblical truths. They saw that this book built precept upon precept in teaching children the great principles and facts of the Christian faith.

In turn, my mother used this book in our preschool and elementary training. She not only read it to us and quizzed us with questions following each story, she also taught us this was a book to be loved. It gave us an early appreciation for the Bible and told us of the historical examples to follow as we grew up.

It was a memorable day when I received my own copy of *First Steps for Little Feet Along Gospel Paths*. I cherished the little book. I could not read yet, but I remember gently leafing through the book, looking at the pictures and anticipating the day when I could read it myself.

When my own children were ready for family prayer time, we proceeded with gusto. I went to the store and bought all the new Bible storybooks, books on how to have exciting family devotions, and idea books. For the first few days, things went fairly well, but eventually the plan fizzled.

Finally, I remembered *First Steps for Little Feet Along Gospel Paths* on my bookshelf. My children had been delighted to see my name scrawled in pencil in the front. They were excited about a book their Mommy read when she was little and even their Tai Tai (what they called my Mother; pronounced Teddy, meaning "old lady" in Chinese) read when she was a little girl in China.

My children enjoyed the short stories. The family devotion time took us a total of about ten minutes. My three-and-a-half-year-old daughter thought it was great and did very well. And even though my two-year-old son didn't answer the questions, he was learning from his sister.

Updating

As we progressed through the book, it became increasingly clear that the book needed updating. The language of the 1800s sounded strange to us. The concept of the book was still excellent—it was a classic. So I began to edit words and phrases as I went along.

On a visit home to my parents' home in North Carolina one Easter in the late 1970s, I told my mother that the book needed to be rewritten and suggested that she do it. But she turned around and said that she thought I should do it. As I continued to edit, rewrite, and add some original material, I became aware of the value of this book as a tool in

teaching children. Mr. Foster's concept of building upon a foundation, precept upon precept, was strong. And when I double-checked a fact in Scripture, I was impressed with the accuracy of the book. It was an exciting project for me.

Thus came the publication of the 1980 edition, called *First Steps in the Bible*.

Over 25 years after the 1980 edition released, I once again revised stories, added new ones, and removed weak stories. You have the newest edition of the classic book in your hands: *Step into the Bible*. The title represents the interactive features that encourage families to develop their faith during devotional time.

A Unique Book

As you go through this book with your children, you will notice that it is far from being a surface Bible storybook. Through Bible stories, I introduce the basic doctrines, obedience to God, original sin, Christ's atoning death, and eternal life. Children understand these principles and readily accept them. It is easy for adults to make things too complicated. Children want to believe and have such open hearts toward God.

Over 300 full-color illustrations and photographs will capture your children's imaginations. Also, throughout the book there are Parent Notes to help you guide your children into an understanding of the principles set forth.

Every story has an appropriate Memory Verse. I feel it is important for children to begin memorizing verses early to become a lifelong habit. Questions follow each story, which help both children and adults learn about themselves, their faith, and God.

Devotions for the Family

When I was growing up, we had family prayers right after breakfast. I found that a good time for my children was right after dinner. Things didn't seem quite so rushed, and we were all together and refreshed by a good meal. It is important to keep things short—only ten to fifteen minutes. Try to be regular and consistent.

How to Start

Read a story, ask the questions, and then have a short prayer. If you have very young children, the questions might be a bit difficult and you may want to rephrase them so that the answer is in the question.

When it comes to the prayer time, on some occasions my children liked to have short sentence prayers so that each in turn could pray out loud. Remember to teach your children to praise and thank the Lord first. Always be specific in your requests as well as in your praise. Perhaps you could begin a family prayer list which would include friends, teachers, schoolwork, pastor, missionaries, world leaders, and others. When you see answers, be sure to point them out to your children and talk about how good God is to answer our prayers.

Expect to have squirming and wiggling and a few interruptions when you are reading to little ones. It is surprising how much they absorb even while squirming. Don't make it a pressured competitive situation. If a child cannot answer a question or has not listened very well, don't worry. They will probably get it the next time around. With 100 stories, you have many opportunities!

Family Togetherness Time

I loved reading to my children! It was a wonderful way to spend concentrated time with them. Now I love reading to my grandchildren.

Reading can also spark marvelous conversations with your children. Learn to listen to them. Try to make your reading exciting by voice inflection. (My mother had such a wonderful Scottish brogue and my grandmother could imitate all the Southern accents.) Use this book as a catalyst for family time; gather together for a time of fun and spiritual training. You will be surprised what this will lead to in family growth and closeness. God will bless your efforts.

A Book to Enjoy

Step into the Bible does not have to be limited to family devotions. Place it where it can be easily reached for little ones to look at on their own, or for older children to read to themselves. Let them use it as a reference book for Sunday school lessons.

It is a book to be used and enjoyed by the whole family. While your aim as parents may be to use it for spiritual development in your children, they don't have to be aware of that!

My mother used to say, "The best way to get a child to eat his vegetables is to have him see his parents enjoying their vegetables." So it is with spiritual training!

And so, you have in your hands a unique book that has stood the test of time and that has contributed to the nurturing of four generations of Grahams. It is a classic. The revisions have enhanced Charles Foster's original book by adding:

- Over 300 photographs and illustrations that will expand a child's world through color, art, geography, and culture. Contemporary photographs portraying biblical themes and situations will help bring the Bible closer to your children.
- Memory Verses to help establish a lifelong habit.
- Bible references so that you can refer back to Scripture.
- Questions at the end of each story to bring the Bible into your child's world.
- Parent Notes to offer you tips or advice.

It is my prayer that you enjoy this book together, and that God will use it to draw your family not only closer to each other but also closer to Him.

Ruth Graham

step 1

The LORD God Made It All

Genesis 1:3–5; 14–19; 26–27

My family had a pet bird when my children were growing up. His name was Red. My son named him that to be silly—the bird was yellow! The birdcage used to hang in my kitchen. It was very shiny and shaped like a Japanese house. I remember when we bought it at the store. A man made the cage so he could sell it. People can make cages, chairs, cars, houses, and many, many other things, but they can't make birds or things that are alive. Only God can create life.

Did you know God made you, too? You are very special to Him; He loves you and cares about you.

God lives in heaven. We cannot see Him, but He sees us all the time, even at night.

You get ready for bed and get tucked in. Pretty soon the moon comes out and the stars twinkle up in the sky.

God made the sun and the moon and the stars up in the sky. He made everything. God is amazing.

Questions

- Who made the birdcage?
- Who makes things that are alive?
- Where does God live?
- When can God see us?
- Who else did God make?

Memory Verse

In the beginning God created the heavens and the earth.

Genesis 1:1

Seasons Change

Genesis 1:6–8

On a pretty spring day, I love to lie down in the grass and watch the clouds float along in the sky. One summer my granddaughter and I walked the beach and had a grand time imagining shapes in the clouds.

God made those clouds.

Sometimes they bring rain and, up north, the clouds sometimes bring snow in the wintertime. When I lived up north, it was fun to get up in the morning and discover that during the night, snow had covered the ground. We bundled up in coats, hats, boots, and gloves to go play outside. And when my children were young, we made a special kind of maple candy that we only made when it snowed.

God made the rain and snow that comes down from the clouds.

After the snow melts in springtime, I like to go out to where I know flowers usually grow. They start growing up from the dirt even under the snow. They know when to begin to grow. God tells them when.

I love springtime when the birds sing again, the grass grows green, and the leaves come back on the trees. And I like to watch the big fat robins hopping about on the lawn snatching up worms.

Questions

- What do we see up in the sky besides the sun, moon, and stars?
- What do clouds bring?
- After the snow melts what comes up from the ground?
- Who tells them to come up?

Memory Verse

In the beginning God created the heavens and the earth.

Genesis 1:1

God Made the Fish

Genesis 1:20–23

When my children were little, we had a black and white cat. We named her Momma Cat because she had five kittens under my bed! We also had a small fish bowl where we kept the fish my children won at a school fair.

Momma Cat always drank water from that bowl. She never bothered the fish, though. We finally decided that the water must have had a fish flavor!

Fish can also live in streams and rivers, oceans and lakes, or maybe a pond in your backyard, like I have now.

Fish don't have feet or legs like animals, or wings like birds. Instead, God gave them fins so they could swim in the water. And they have a special way of breathing—through gills—so they can stay in the water all the time.

There are many kinds of fish. Some are very small and some have beautiful colors. Some are very big and some are funny looking. Some fish we never see because they live at the bottom of the ocean.

God made all the fish and everything in the oceans. He made the beautiful goldfish and also the huge whale. He takes care of them and has given them all they need to live in the water.

Questions

- Who made the fish?
- Do they have wings and feet?
- What do they have instead?
- Where did God make the fish live?
- Did God give them all they need to live in the water?

Memory Verse

In the beginning God created the heavens and the earth.

Genesis 1:1

God Made the Animals

Genesis 1:24–25

My grandson loves animals—all kinds of animals! One summer we went to the zoo. We saw baby white tigers, baboons, and flamingoes. My grandson even got to ride an elephant!

Did you know that God made all the animals? Some animals are wild and live out in the woods or jungle, like wolves, bears, and tigers. Other animals are tame, like sheep and cows.

If you've been to the zoo, you've seen lots of different kinds of animals. The wild animals are usually in a cage so they can't hurt us or people can't hurt them. The tame animals are put in a special area so we can pet them.

Tigers and lions are very fierce and could hurt us, but they live in countries very far from here. Or maybe you live where they do! We can go see them in the zoo, where we are protected from them, or we can look at pictures of them. They are very beautiful and strong animals.

God also made zebras with their black and white stripes. He made giraffes with their long legs and blue tongues! He made cheetahs that run very fast and sloths that move very slowly. God made all kinds of different animals.

Questions

- Who made the animals?
- Have you been to a zoo?
- Which animal do you like best?

Memory Verse

In the beginning God created the
heavens and the earth.

Genesis 1:1

step 5

God Made People

Genesis 1:26–28

You live on a big planet called the earth. And lots and lots of other people live on it, too.

Maybe there are many families on your street. There are streets like yours all over the earth. There are so many people we can hardly count them.

God made this earth and gave us everything we need to live. He provided it for us to enjoy because He loves us. He does not want us to destroy or neglect it. We must take care of what He gave us and try to keep it beautiful.

Where you live, there are probably some people whose skin is a different color from yours or whose eyes are a different shape. And maybe you know someone who speaks in a language that sounds strange to you because you don't understand it. They might come from another country—maybe even the other side of the earth! The earth is a big place.

Even with all the people on the earth, no one is the same. We are all special in the way we act, look, and think. Do you know what? God made us that way, and He loves us all.

Parent Note: In this step I wanted to establish an awareness of the need to care for this beautiful world God gave us to enjoy. You may want to further the discussion on practical matters such as recycling and not littering.

Questions

- What is the name of the planet where we live?
- Are there lots of people on the earth who live here?
- Who made us?
- What are some things you can do to help keep God's earth beautiful?

Memory Verse

In the beginning God created the heavens and the earth.

Genesis 1:1

step 6

Paradise Lost

Genesis 2:15–3:19

Sometimes, especially in the spring or fall, when you are riding in the car with your mother or father, you may see a squirrel or bird that has been hit by a car and killed. It makes me sad when I see it.

Maybe you say to your mom, "God will make it all better," or you might ask, "Wasn't God taking care of that bird or squirrel?"

The answer to that started a long time ago. After God made the world and all the birds, animals, and fish, He looked around and said something was missing. He decided to make a man named Adam. And he did. Then God gave Adam a woman to be his wife—Eve—so he wouldn't be all by himself.

God was very happy that He made Adam and Eve. He put them in a beautiful garden, called Eden, that was full of wonderful plants and animals and birds. Everything was perfect. No one cried or was sick or died. All the animals loved each other. No one hurt anyone else. God gave Adam and Eve everything they needed and told them to enjoy everything. But He told them that there was fruit on one tree in the garden that they could not eat. He told them that they must obey Him.

Everything was great until one day when Eve began to talk with a slithery snake—which was Satan in disguise. He questioned what God had told her about the fruit tree. Soon Satan convinced Eve that it wasn't as important to obey God as she had thought, so she ate some of the fruit from that tree. She gave some to Adam, too.

All of a sudden they realized that they had been very wrong to listen to Satan and disobey God. When they heard God coming in the garden, they hid.

God was very sad because He knew what Adam and Eve had done. They had disobeyed Him—that is called a sin. God knew He would have to punish them.

Part of the punishment was death. Sin always ends in death.

Ever since Adam and Eve sinned by disobeying God, people, animals, birds, and fish have died.

But God has provided a wonderful way for us to live forever. He sent His Son Jesus to take the punishment for us so that when we die we can go to heaven and live forever. All we have to do is ask Jesus into our hearts to wash away our sins, and He does! Isn't that exciting?

Parent Note: This story contains many concepts: the reality of Satan and his efforts to get us to disobey God, penalty for disobeying God, the atoning death of Christ, eternal life, and original sin. Children accept these things so easily and do not question them. Do not make it complicated, just present it as it is.

Questions

- Was the garden of Eden perfect?
- What did God tell Adam and Eve not to do?
- Who did Satan make Eve doubt?
- What did Adam and Eve do?
- What was the punishment?
- When Adam and Eve sinned, why did that affect everyone else ever to be born?

Memory Verse

I will maintain my love to him forever, and my covenant to him will never fail.

Psalm 89:28

step 7

New Hope

Genesis 6–9

Not long ago a movie was being filmed near my house. For the movie they built an ark—a big boat. Then the actors and all sorts of animals—giraffes, elephants, lions—went into it. It was all for a movie—like make believe.

But let me tell you about the real ark. Noah was a good man. He obeyed God even though those around him did not. God decided to punish them.

God said He was going to send a flood to cover the whole world to destroy the ones who did not obey God. He told Noah to build an ark, how big He wanted it to be, and what animals to bring into the ark. God was going to send a lot of rain, but He promised Noah that He would take care of them.

Even though it might not have rained in a long time and his neighbors might have made fun of him, Noah did obey. He built the ark.

When the ark was finished, God told Noah to go inside with his family and all the animals.

God shut the door and then it began to rain. It rained for forty days and forty nights. Water covered everything. Soon the ark began to float—higher than the houses, trees, mountains! Everything that had been living on land died underwater.

But Noah, his family, and all the animals were safe inside the ark.

Then the rain stopped and the flood waters began to go down. The ark came to rest on a mountain. But they couldn't leave the ark because water was still everywhere.

After the flood waters dried up, God told Noah and his family they could leave the ark with the animals, and stand once again on dry ground.

When they left the ark, Noah and his family first took time to worship God and thank him for his protection. God promised that He would never again cause a flood to cover the whole earth. As a sign of this covenant, or promise, God made a rainbow.

Questions

- Who told Noah to build the ark? Why?

- How would you have felt to be on the ark with all those animals for so long?

- When Noah and his family left the ark, what was the first thing they did?

- What did God promise Noah?

- What was the sign that He would keep his promise?

- What was the difference between Noah and his neighbors?

This is Mt. Ararat in Armenia, near Turkey. Some people think the ark landed here.

Memory Verse

I will maintain my love to him forever, and my covenant to him will never fail.

Psalm 89:28

Abraham Follows God's Plan

Genesis 12:1–8

Have you ever moved from your home? If you did, you had to pack up your toys, clothes, books, and say good-bye to all your friends. That is hard to do. I have moved several times and I have never learned to like it. Can you imagine packing up your things and leaving, but you didn't know where you were going?

Ever since Adam and Eve had to leave the garden of Eden, God planned to redeem, or rescue, people from their sin. In this plan, He chose a group of people who would be the family of Jesus. This family began with a man named Abraham.

A long time ago God told Abraham to leave his home, family, friends, and country to go to a place God would show him. Abraham had no idea where he would go. God promised to make Abraham's family into a great nation.

That must have been a hard decision for Abraham to leave everything, but he obeyed God. He did what God told him to do even though he didn't know where he was going. That is called faith—to obey even though you don't know what is going to happen to you.

Abraham took his wife, Sarah, his nephew, and everything he owned, including his cattle, sheep, camels, and servants. They traveled where God led. It wasn't an easy trip through the desert, but he was determined to follow God's plan.

When he got to the place, God promised to give him the land—even though others were living there. Abraham believed God and took time to worship Him.

Abraham had no idea what his obedience would mean, but you and I have been affected by Abraham's decision to obey God. Through Abraham, all people would be saved. Jesus would be born into that family many years later. Because of Jesus, our sins can be forgiven and we can all know God. What a wonderful gift!

Questions

- What did God ask Abraham to do?
- What did God promise Abraham?
- What did Abraham do when he got to Canaan?
- Do you think it is important to obey God?
- What is faith?

Memory Verse

I will maintain my love to him forever, and my covenant to him will never fail.

Psalm 89:28

I will love him be kind to him
forever; my covenant w/ him will
never end.

step 9

A Mother and Son Are Saved

Genesis 21:14–21

God not only made all the different kinds of people and animals in the world to love, but He also made wonderful creatures called angels. Angels are God's messengers. Everyone who believes in Jesus has an angel all to himself or herself. Angels take care of us; they are often called guardian angels.

When angels are not busy taking care of people or doing other things for God, they live in heaven. Angels are very good and obey God when He tells them to do something.

A very long time ago, there was a little boy named Ishmael. His mother's name was Hagar. They lived in a tent (people lived in tents then), but they were told they had to leave their home. Ishmael and Hagar were sad, but they packed their things and left.

They had no place to go, so they wandered out into the desert. A desert is a place where practically no one lives. It isn't a very nice place. It can get very hot.

Pretty soon, little Ishmael got thirsty. His mother gave him some water, but then they ran out. They looked and looked for more water but couldn't find any. Ishmael got very weak. Hagar saw that he was going to die unless he got some water soon. She put him under a bush in the shade where it wasn't as hot.

She was very sad and walked away because she didn't want to see him die. She began to cry.

Then God sent an angel to her. The angel asked, "What is the matter, Hagar? Do not be afraid; God has heard the boy crying as he lies there. Lift the boy up and take him by the hand…" Then the angel brought her to a well.

So Hagar quickly got Ishmael some water to drink. He got strong and well. He grew up to be a man and lived in the desert.

Parent Note: If you would like to find out more about angels and what they do, let me refer you to *Angels: God's Secret Agents* by Billy Graham.

Questions

- Where do angels live when they aren't taking care of people or doing other things for God?
- Why was Ishmael so sick?
- Why did Hagar walk away?
- What did the angel show Hagar?

Memory Verse

I will maintain my love to him forever, and my covenant to him will never fail.

Psalm 89:28

The Priestly Blessing

Numbers 6:22–27

The LORD said to Moses,
"Tell Aaron and his sons, 'This is how you are to bless the
Israelites. Say to them:
" ' "The LORD bless you and keep you;
the LORD make his face shine upon you
and be gracious to you;
the LORD turn his face toward you
and give you peace." '
"So they will put my name on the Israelites,
and I will bless them."

Questions

- Who is speaking in this passage?
- Who is this a blessing for?
- What do you think this passage means?

Memory Verse

I will maintain my love to him forever, and my covenant to him will never fail.

Psalm 89:28

Angels on a Stairway

Genesis 28:10–22

When you sleep do you dream? In the morning when you wake up, do you remember what you dreamed? Sometimes dreams are very important.

Jacob was in trouble. He had lied to his father, Isaac, and stolen from his brother, Esau. His mother, Rebekah, told him to stay with his uncle until things cooled down. He was really afraid of what his brother might do to him. So he took off.

He traveled far away. The sun had gone down and he was tired. He found a good spot to lay down. He used a rock for his pillow! He was so tired, he went to sleep.

Jacob had a very important dream. He dreamed there was a stairway that went all the way up into heaven. He could see angels going up and down the stairway. At the very top was God. He told Jacob that he was the God of his grandfather, Abraham, and his father, Isaac.

God promised to give Jacob and his children the land where he was sleeping. God said Jacob's family was going to be very big—hundreds and thousands of people. And because of his children, other people would be blessed. God promised to watch over him and bring him back home.

Jacob woke up early and remembered his dream. He realized that God had been there even though he had not been aware of it. He named the place where he had the dream "Bethel," which means "house of God."

This was going to be a very special place for Jacob and his family.

While he was there, he promised that he would serve God and give a tenth of all that God gave him.

Parent Note: The principle of tithing is very important. Introducing it early can make it a life-time habit. God blesses us when we give him ten percent of what we have.

Questions

- Is there a time when you felt God very close to you?

- God made promises to Jacob. He has made promises in the Bible to you. Can you think of any?

- Do you give to God?

Memory Verse

Do not forget my teaching, but keep my commands in your heart.

Proverbs 3:1

step 12

Trouble With Brothers

Genesis 37

I have two older sisters and two younger brothers. When we were growing up, we fought a lot. Sometimes I wished I could get rid of one of them. Have you ever felt that way?

Joseph's brothers hated him because he was their father's favorite son. One day their father gave Joseph a bright, colorful coat. None of the other boys had a coat like that. They hated Joseph even more.

Joseph liked to tell his brothers about his dreams. One of his dreams was about them bundling up grain in the field. His bundle stood up tall while his brothers' bundles bowed down to his. They asked if he was going to rule over them. In another, he dreamed that the sun, moon, and stars all bowed down to him. This made his brothers angry.

One day his brothers were tending sheep in the fields. Jacob sent Joseph out to find out if they were okay. When his brothers saw him coming, they planned to kill him. But the oldest brother didn't think that was a good idea. Instead he told them to put Joseph in a deep pit, thinking he could rescue Joseph later. When Joseph arrived, his brothers took his clothes and the beautiful coat their father had given him. They threw him in the pit. Then they sat down to eat.

Soon they saw a group of travelers coming by on their way to Egypt. The brothers decided to sell him to the travelers.

They took Joseph's beautiful coat and dipped it in blood so it would look like Joseph had been attacked by an animal. They took the bloody coat to their father and lied about what happened to Joseph.

Questions

- Why were Joseph's brothers so mad at him?
- What did they do to Joseph?
- What did they say happened to Joseph?
- What was the truth?

Jacob was very sad because he thought Joseph was dead. No one could comfort him.

But that isn't the end of the story! You'll find out what happened to Joseph in the next story.

Parent Note: Favoritism in a family is harmful. It creates insecurities, bitterness, jealousy, and unhealthy attitudes. We see this in the stories of Jacob and Joseph. Ask God to show you if you have a favorite child. Ask Him to help you love and treat your children equally. They are special in their own right and God has unique plans for them.

Memory Verse

Do not forget my teaching, but keep my commands in your heart.

Proverbs 3:1

Dreams Come True

Genesis 39–50

In the last story, you learned that Joseph's brothers sold him to some travelers going far away to Egypt. His brothers thought they had seen the last of him.

Although Joseph may have been afraid and alone without his family, God was with him. His new boss saw that God was helping Joseph, so he put Joseph in charge of his house. It was a big job but Joseph did it well.

His new boss' wife was not a nice lady. She said terrible things about Joseph, so he was put in jail. But God was still with Joseph. He soon was put in charge of all the other prisoners.

One day, two new men were put into the jail. They had made the king very mad. He put them in the same jail as Joseph.

While in jail the two men had two different dreams on the same night. They told Joseph about them. With God's help Joseph told them what their dreams meant. Both of the men's dreams came true.

One night the king had two dreams. He didn't know what they meant. He asked all the smartest men what his dreams meant. But they didn't know. Then one of the men who had known Joseph in jail remembered something. Joseph could tell them what the dreams meant.

With God's help, Joseph told the king what they meant. Joseph told the king that there were going to be seven good years and seven bad years. He advised the king to use the good years to prepare for the bad years. When the bad years came they were ready. Soon people came from all over to ask the Egyptians for food. It all happened just as Joseph said it would.

The king was so happy with Joseph that he put him in charge of his whole kingdom. The only person more important than Joseph was the king himself.

Guess who came to Egypt looking for food. Joseph's brothers! They had no idea that their little brother was now so powerful in Egypt. They didn't recognize him. They came and bowed down to him. (Remember the dream he told his brothers about them bowing down to him? Joseph's dream had come true after all these years.)

He knew who they were but didn't let them know. He wanted to see if they had changed. They were afraid of this important man.

After many days he showed them who he was.

Questions

- During everything that happened to Joseph, who was with him?
- Who gave Joseph wisdom?
- What would you have done to your brothers?
- What did Joseph do?
- Why is forgiveness so important?

Joseph told them not to be afraid because God had sent him to Egypt so that they would have food during the bad years. God was making sure their family would survive. He said, "You intended to harm me, but God intended it for good to accomplish what is now being done, the saving of many lives."

Joseph forgave his brothers and hugged them.

When the king heard that Joseph's brothers had come, he was very happy. The king told them to bring the rest of Jacob's family to Egypt so that he could take care of them.

And that is what they did!

Memory Verse

Do not forget my teaching, but keep my commands in your heart.

Proverbs 3:1

step 14

Baby for the Princess

Exodus 2:1–10

I have a new baby grandson. The first time he visited me I prepared a cradle for him. I lined it with clean padding and pretty blue fabric. I placed a little mattress in the bottom so it would be soft. I wanted it to be just right.

Remember the story about Joseph becoming an important man in Egypt? After Joseph died, a new king, called a pharaoh, came to power—one that did not know Joseph. He saw that Joseph's family had become too large and powerful so he ordered all Hebrew baby boys to be killed. He was a very wicked pharaoh.

Moses was a baby boy. His mom loved him very much and didn't want him to be killed. She decided to hide him from the pharaoh. When she couldn't hide Moses at home any longer she prepared a basket for him. She made sure it was tight and safe. Maybe she even padded it like I did the cradle. She then put him in the basket and hid the basket in the reeds along the Nile River. It was like a little basket boat! Moses' mother asked his sister to stay nearby to watch over him in the basket.

One day the Pharaoh's daughter, a princess, went down to take a bath in the river. She discovered the basket in the reeds and peeked inside. There was baby Moses! He was crying and she felt sorry for him. "He must be a Hebrew baby," she said.

Moses' sister quickly asked the princess, "Shall I go and get one of the Hebrew women to take care of the baby for you?"

"Yes, go," the princess agreed. Moses' sister went home and got her mom. Moses' mom took him home with her and watched over him until he grew a little older. Then she took him back to the princess. He grew up in the palace as if he were a member of Pharaoh's own family.

Questions

- Why did the pharaoh want all the baby boys killed?

- What did Moses' mom do?

- Who watched over Moses?

- What happened to Moses?

Memory Verse

Do not forget my teaching, but keep my commands in your heart.

Proverbs 3:1

God's Message to Moses

Exodus 3–14

I like to watch funny DVDs. My favorite ones are about animals that seem to talk. It's funny because it is so unexpected.

While Moses was tending sheep he noticed a nearby bush was on fire. This was a strange thing—a bush that was on fire but wasn't burning up! Moses went closer to see what was happening. As he got closer, God called his name from out of the bush, "Moses! Moses!"

Moses answered God and said, "Here I am."

God told Moses not to come any closer and to take off his shoes because this was a special place. Moses hid his face because he was afraid to look at God. He told Moses that He was the God of Abraham, Isaac, and Jacob. He had seen the troubles of His people, who were now slaves in Egypt. He had heard their prayers.

Then God said that He was going to send Moses back to Egypt to tell the new pharaoh to let the slaves go.

The slaves finally escaped, and Moses led them out of Egypt. But they weren't safe yet. Pharaoh and his army were close behind Moses and God's people.

Soon they came to the Red Sea. To get away from the army, God told Moses to raise his staff over the Red Sea to make a path. Moses and God's people followed the path through the sea safely to the other shore. Moses raised his staff again, and the rushing water swept away Pharaoh and his army. Then Moses led the people to a place that God had promised Abraham so long ago. God keeps His promises.

Questions

- What did Moses see in the desert?
- Whose voice did he hear?
- How does God talk to you?
- Had God heard and seen the troubles of His people?
- What did God tell Moses he was going to do?

Memory Verse

Do not forget my teaching, but keep my commands in your heart.

Proverbs 3:1

We're So Hungry

Exodus 16—17:6

Moses and the Israelites walked through the desert for days and days. They were traveling to the Promised Land—and they couldn't wait to get there. The desert was dry and dusty. They were getting tired of this trip. They began to long for the things they had in Egypt.

Soon, people started grumbling that there wasn't anything to eat in the desert.

"If we were still in Egypt, we'd have plenty to eat!" someone complained.

"We are starving!" another whined.

God heard their cries. That night, He sent meat in the form of birds called quail for the Israelites to eat. The next morning, he sent bread called manna so that they wouldn't starve.

Moses and the Israelites kept walking and walking, farther and farther. They probably asked Moses, "Are we there yet?" They wondered if they'd ever get there. They started grumbling again. "Why did you bring us up out of Egypt to make us and our children and livestock die of thirst?" someone complained.

"We are thirsty!" another whined.

Moses didn't know what to do. The Israelites and their animals were so thirsty! There was no water in the desert. Moses prayed to God for help.

God led Moses to a rock. God said, "Strike the rock, and water will come out of it for the people to drink."

Whooooosh!

Water gushed from the dry rock like a fountain. The Israelites all had enough drink. Isn't God amazing?

Questions

- Where were the Israelites traveling to?
- What did the Israelites eat at night?
- What did the Israelites eat in the morning?
- Who sent them their food?
- What came out of a rock?
- Who made the water come out of the rock?

Memory Verse

Trust in the LORD with all your heart and lean not on your own understanding.

Proverbs 3:5

God's Rules

Exodus 20:3–17

God made all the people in the world, and He loves us. He also wants us to love and help each other. But because we want to do bad things more than we want to do good things, He gave us a set of rules. These rules are called the Ten Commandments.

1. You should only worship God.
2. Do not create anything that you think looks like God or that you treat like God.
3. Always behave in a way that shows love and respect for God.
4. One day of the week should be saved for rest and worshiping God.
5. Obey your parents and be respectful toward them.
6. You must respect life.
7. When people get married, husbands and wives must only share that special love with each other.
8. Do not take anything that does not belong to you.
9. Do not lie—always tell the truth.
10. You shouldn't want something so badly that you would do anything to get it.

These are very important rules. But no one can keep them perfectly. Only one Person ever kept them and that was Jesus. When we read these rules we see that we need forgiveness for what we have done wrong. To ask forgiveness means to say we are sorry and will try not to do them anymore. God is always ready to forgive us.

Parent Note: It may seem strange to include a story on the Ten Commandments in a book for children. But in this age in which relativity and situational ethics have been enthroned, it is vital for a child to know that there are some absolutes and a moral code given by God. My mother used the illustration of a highway without painted traffic lanes. No one would know where they were supposed to drive – and all would be havoc. So it is morally and spiritually. God has given us a standard of excellence.

Questions

- Why did God give us these rules?
- Can you name a few?
- Who kept all these commandments perfectly?
- If we know we have done wrong, what can we ask God to do?
- Will He forgive us?
- How can you tell if you love something or someone more than God?

לא תרצח
לא תנאף
לא תגנב
לא תענה
לא תחמד

אנכי יהוה
לא יהיה
לא תשא את
זכור את יום
כבד את אביך

Memory Verse

Trust in the LORD with all your heart and lean not on your own understanding.

Proverbs 3:5

Spying the New Land

Numbers 13:1–14:9

Do you like to explore? When I was a little girl, my sister, Anne, and I would explore the woods around our house. We would find all kinds of "treasures" in our woods.

The children of Israel were at the border of the new land—the new home God had promised Abraham a long time ago. God told Moses to send explorers into the land to see what it was like. He sent out twelve explorers.

Moses told them to go throughout the country to see if the land was good and what the people were like there. Were they strong? Weak? Few? Many? He wanted to know what kind of towns the people lived in and if they were well guarded. He wanted to know if the land was good for farming. Moses wanted to know all the details before sending the Israelites.

He asked the explorers to bring back samples of the fruits of the land. It was grape season so he asked them to bring back some grapes. Maybe grapes were Moses' favorite fruit!

The explorers traveled all over the country. When they reached the vineyard, they cut off a big bunch of grapes—it was so big that two men had to carry it on a pole between them! They went back to Moses to report what they had seen.

The explorers told him it was a good place where they could grow plenty of food. They also told Moses that the people who lived there were very strong and the towns well protected. Ten of the twelve explorers were afraid and did not want the Israelites to go into the land. The Israelites listened to these explorers. The people became afraid and very upset. But two of the explorers, Joshua and Caleb, disagreed with the others and said that they should make the land their home.

Joshua stood up and told them that the land was very good. He reminded the Israelites that God had promised to give them the land. Joshua and Caleb urged the Israelites not to disobey God and not be afraid. God was on their side.

Parent Note: This story can give you the opportunity to talk about peer pressure. "My son, if sinners entice you, do not give into them." (Proverbs 1:10) My mother's version of that verse was: "If bad boys tell you to do bad things, say no." It seems really hard at first, but God helps us just say no.

Questions

- How many explorers did Moses send?
- What did they see in the new land?
- What did they tell Moses?
- What did Joshua and Caleb say?
- Who did they say was on their side?
- Do you think it was hard for Joshua and Caleb to stand up and disagree with the other ten explorers?

Memory Verse

Trust in the LORD with all your heart and lean not on your own understanding.

Proverbs 3:5

step 19

A New Home

Joshua 1:1–9; 21:44–45; 23:1–11

In school when it was time for a test, I would get very nervous. I would worry that I hadn't studied enough; that I wouldn't know the right answers. But then I remembered that the Bible says we are not to worry about anything because God is with us. I kept thinking about that. God's promise helped me.

The same was true for Joshua. God had a big job for him. Moses had died, so God told Joshua that he was now the new leader. There would be many hard days ahead, but God said to remember His Word.

God promised He would give them the land just as He had promised Moses. Although they must have been very sad that Moses was dead, it was also an exciting time. They had traveled in the desert a long time and now they were about to enter the land that God had promised Abraham years before. God keeps His promises!

God said He would be with Joshua just as He had been with Moses. He would never leave Joshua's side and Joshua would never have to be afraid. God told Joshua to be strong and brave and obey Him.

He told Joshua to think about God's Word all the time—to talk about God's Word. He was to make God's Word the most important thing in his life.

Just as God promised, He was with Joshua as they moved into their new home. It was not easy. Joshua, with God's help, was able to start a new home for the people of Israel.

Questions

- What did God promise Joshua?
- What did God tell Joshua to do?
- Did Joshua obey?
- What happened to Joshua and the people of Israel?

Memory Verse

Trust in the LORD with all your heart and lean not on your own understanding.

Proverbs 3:5

step 20

Fly Like an Eagle

Isaiah 40:28–31

> The LORD is the everlasting God,
> the Creator of the ends of the earth.
> He will not grow tired or weary,
> and his understanding no one can fathom.
> He gives strength to the weary
> and increases the power of the weak.
> Even youths grow tired and weary,
> and young men stumble and fall;
> but those who hope in the LORD
> will renew their strength.
> They will soar on wings like eagles;
> they will run and not grow weary,
> they will walk and not be faint.

Questions

- What did God create?
- Who does God help?
- What can we do if we need help?

Memory Verse

Trust in the LORD with all your heart and lean not on your own understanding.

Proverbs 3:5

step 21

Called by Name

1 Samuel 1–3

Have you ever had to give back something you loved very much? I have.

Maybe you were taking care of your friend's dog for the summer. But when your friend came home you didn't want to give him back. You had fallen in love with the dog and wanted to keep him. But you gave him back.

Hannah was very sad because she wanted a baby more than anything in the world. She went to God's house to pray very hard that God would give her a little boy. She promised God that if He gave her a little boy, she would give him back to God. That meant he would grow up in God's house learning to serve God and others.

God answered her prayer! She had a baby boy and named him Samuel. Hannah remembered the promise she made to God. Hannah and her husband took him to God's house. He lived with Eli, the priest. His parents visited him each year. She loved Samuel very much.

As Samuel grew up, he did what was right and pleased God. He was getting tall and everyone liked him.

One night Samuel heard someone call his name, "Samuel." He thought it must be Eli so he went to Eli, but Eli told him he had not called. Eli sent him back to bed. Again, Samuel heard someone call his name, "Samuel." Samuel went to Eli and said, "Here I am. You called me." But again Eli told him that he had not called. Once more he heard a voice call, "Samuel." Again he went to Eli. This time Eli knew God was calling Samuel. Eli said to go back to bed and when it happened again say, "Speak LORD, for your servant is listening."

This time when he heard, "Samuel! Samuel!" instead of going to Eli, Samuel said, "Speak for your servant is listening."

Samuel learned to listen for God's voice and obey God. He grew up to become a great prophet. God was with him.

Questions

- What did Hannah ask God for?
- What did she promise God?
- Did she keep her promise?
- Even though Samuel was a little boy, who called him?

Memory Verse

"… Set an example for the believers in speech, in life, in faith and purity."
1 Timothy 4:12

step 22

An Unlikely Cure

2 Kings 5:1–14

While Israel and another country were fighting, a little girl was taken from her home. She missed her home, but she loved and trusted God. Eventually she learned to love the new people and her new home. The people did not know or love God.

This little girl worked for a family. Naaman, the father, was very sick. The little girl was sad that he was so sick. She told Naaman's wife that back in her old home, a great prophet, named Elisha, could cure him.

Naaman went to the king to get permission to go to Israel. The king said yes.

So Naaman went to Elisha's house, but Elisha didn't come out to meet him. He sent a messenger, who told him to go wash seven times in the Jordan River, and he would be healed. Naaman got angry. He thought that Elisha was rude not to come out to talk to him. He didn't want to go wash in the Jordan River—it was very muddy. He decided to go back home instead of doing what Elisha said.

On their way back home, one of Naaman's servants asked, "If the prophet had told you to do some great thing would you not have done it? How much more reason, then, to obey him when he tells you, 'wash and be cleansed.' " Naaman realized that this man was right. He turned around and went to the Jordan River.

When he got to the river, it was just as muddy as ever. But he went in and washed once. Nothing happened. Twice, three times—even after he had washed six times—nothing happened. But when he washed the seventh time he was healed. He was completely well, just as Elisha had said. Naaman was very happy.

Naaman went back to Elisha's house to thank him. This time Elisha met him in person. Naaman told Elisha that now he believed in God.

Naaman began to love God because that one little girl, even though she was far from home, still loved and obeyed God.

It took a lot of courage for her to tell Naaman's wife about Elisha and her God, but she trusted God and was not afraid to talk about Him to others.

Parent Note: It is important for children to learn early to talk about Jesus with others. Witnessing is such an important key to our growth as Christians. Children who grow up seeing it done naturally will follow the example. It will lead to a more vital faith.

Questions

- Who told Naaman to go see Elisha?
- What did Elisha tell Naaman to do?
- Why did Naaman go back to Elisha's house?
- What did he tell Elisha?
- Why do you think Naaman was mad that Elisha didn't come to the door the first time?

Memory Verse

"… Set an example for the believers in speech, in life, in faith and purity."
1 Timothy 4:12

This is the Jordan River, where Naaman washed seven times.

Young King

2 Kings 22–23

Josiah was only eight years old when he became king. Can you imagine? Though he was very young, he was a good king who wanted to obey God.

Many in his country had been worshiping idols, or fake gods, instead of the one true God. When Josiah was still young he began to change the way things were being done. Even as a child, Josiah lived differently than the kings who came before him. He tried to live in a way that pleased God. Then as a young man, he began to rebuild the great temple in Jerusalem where the one true God was to be worshiped.

While they were rebuilding the temple, they found God's Law that had been written long before by God through Moses. As they read it they realized that they had been sinning against God by putting other things in God's place.

King Josiah was upset and decided that he and the other people would make a covenant, or promise, to God to obey and do all that God had told them to do. Josiah was going to do this with all his heart and soul. He set an example even though he was young.

The king destroyed all the places where people worshiped other things instead of God. Then they celebrated with a feast in Jerusalem.

Even though King Josiah was young, the Bible tells us, "Neither before nor after Josiah was there a king like him who turned to the LORD as he did—with all his heart and with all his soul and with all his strength."

El-Aksa Mosque in Jerusalem

Questions

- How old was Josiah when he became king?

- Was he a good king?

- What did they find while rebuilding the temple?

- How had the people been sinning against God?

- What did they do about it?

Drawing of a fake god, Baal

Memory Verse

"… Set an example for the believers in speech, in life, in faith and purity."
1 Timothy 4:12

Daniel Faces the Lions

Daniel 6

I like stories about angels and how God sends them to help us. Let me tell you a story about angels.

Once there was a very important king. Everyone had to obey him. He had many lions that he kept in a den.

In the same country there was a very good and wise man named Daniel. But some bad men didn't like Daniel.

These bad men talked the king into making a rule that no one could pray to anyone except him. Anyone who did would be thrown into the lions' den.

But Daniel loved and obeyed God. Daniel prayed to Him three times a day with his window open. Daniel would not pray to the king. The bad men peeked into Daniel's window, then ran to tell the king that he was praying to God.

That made the king sad. The king liked Daniel, but he had made the rule. Now Daniel would have to be thrown into the lions' den. The bad men took Daniel and put him in with the lions. They placed a big stone at the entrance so no one could get out.

The king was worried about Daniel. When the king went to bed later, he couldn't sleep. Early the next morning, he ran to the lions' den to see what had happened to Daniel. He cried out, "Daniel, servant of the living God, has your God, whom you serve continually, been able to rescue you from the lions?" Daniel answered him, "O king, live forever! My God sent his angel, and he shut the mouths of the lions. They have not hurt me."

The king was so happy! He ordered his men to help Daniel out of the den. Everyone could see that Daniel was not hurt at all. God had taken care of him.

Questions

- What did the bad men want to do to Daniel?
- What rule did these men talk the king into making?
- Who did Daniel pray to?
- Whom was sent to help Daniel?
- Is God able to rescue us from danger?
- Why didn't Daniel pray secretly to try to stay out of trouble?

Memory Verse

"… Set an example for the believers in speech, in life, in faith and purity."
1 Timothy 4:12

Jonah Runs Away

Jonah 1–3

Have you ever run away from doing something you were told to do? Maybe your Mom asked you to pick up your toys but you went outside to play with a friend. Did she punish you for disobeying her? Did you have to pick up your toys anyway?

There was a man named Jonah who lived a long time ago. God told him to go to a city named Nineveh and tell the people that they had been doing bad things. God was very unhappy with them. They needed to repent or say they were sorry and quit doing bad things.

Jonah didn't want to do that so he ran away from God. He got on a boat that was going far away.

The boat went way out into the ocean. God made a big storm with wind and waves to toss the boat around. The men on the boat were afraid that it would turn over and they would die.

Jonah was asleep. The captain woke him up and asked him to pray to God to stop the storm. The men on the boat found out the storm was Jonah's fault. They asked him who he was and what he was doing. They became afraid because they realized he was running away from God.

The storm was getting worse. They asked Jonah what they should do. Jonah told them to throw him overboard—then the sea would calm down. The men prayed that they would not die and tossed Jonah into the water. The storm quit and the ocean became calm.

Jonah was in the ocean when a big fish came and swallowed him up! It must have been very dark and smelly inside that fish.

He prayed inside the fish for three days. Jonah did not like it there, so he called out to God for help.

The big fish threw up and out came Jonah onto the beach!

Once again, God told Jonah to go tell the people of Nineveh that they had done bad things and needed to repent.

This time Jonah obeyed. He went to Nineveh and told the people to stop doing bad things. Many people believed in God because of what Jonah told them.

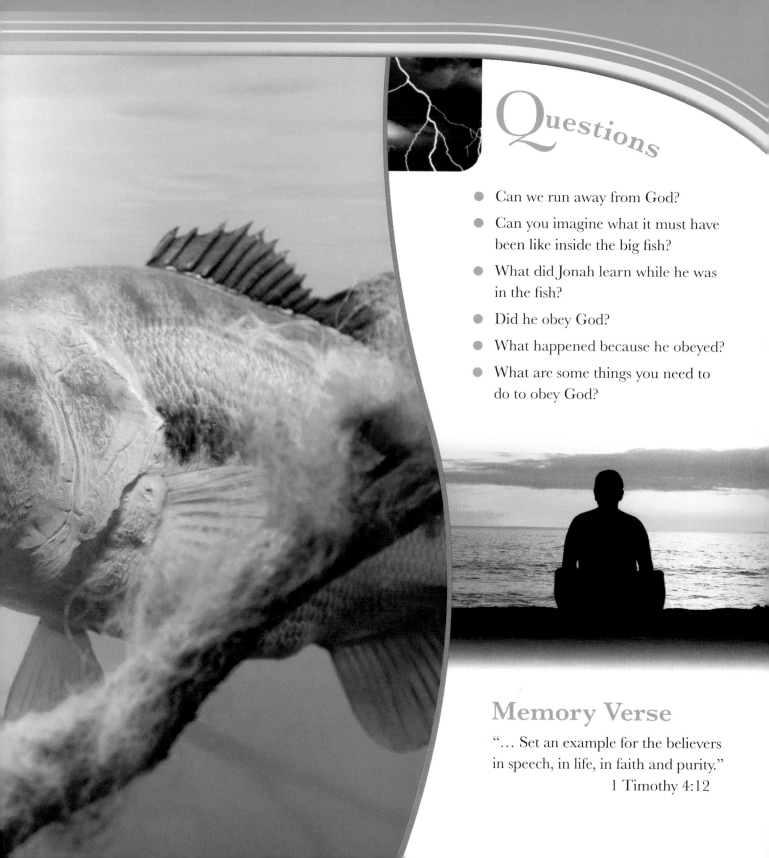

Questions

- Can we run away from God?
- Can you imagine what it must have been like inside the big fish?
- What did Jonah learn while he was in the fish?
- Did he obey God?
- What happened because he obeyed?
- What are some things you need to do to obey God?

Memory Verse

"… Set an example for the believers in speech, in life, in faith and purity."
1 Timothy 4:12

400 Years of Silence

Micah 6:8; Zechariah 1:3

Do you like to get mail? Isn't it fun to go to the mailbox and find something with your name on it? Sometimes I get a letter from someone very special to me and that's even better! But there are times when I don't hear from that special someone and it makes me sad. I wait and wait but nothing comes. I wonder if something has happened to them. Did they go away? Did they quit liking me? Did they forget me? Did something happen to them?

God had given many messages to prophets to tell God's people what He wanted them to do. He wanted them to rebuild the temple and worship Him only. He wanted them to love mercy and walk humbly with Him. There were a few obedient people, but most of them continued to disobey God. They did bad things. He warned them that they would be punished.

And then God got quiet. He didn't say anything to His people for 400 years. That's a long time!

The ones who were obedient were hopeful that God would speak to them again. They hoped year after year. They had no idea how He would speak and He surprised them. He didn't shout from heaven. He didn't stand on a street corner preaching. He didn't send a letter.

He sent a baby—His very own Son!

Questions

- What were God's messengers called?
- Did the people obey?
- How long was God quiet?
- How did God surprise His people?
- Who did He send?

Memory Verse

"For God so loved the world that he gave his one and only Son, that whoever believes in him shall not perish but have eternal life."

John 3:16

step 27

A Special Baby Is Born

Luke 2:1–12

Far away, there is a town called Bethlehem. It is a very old town. Many years ago a young woman named Mary came to Bethlehem with her husband, Joseph. They did not live in Bethlehem, so they had to find an inn where they could spend the night.

The inn was full of people, so Mary and Joseph would not have a room to spend the night. Joseph was sad and a little worried. He needed to find a place for Mary to be comfortable. She was going to have a baby. A special baby.

They went to the stable where the donkeys and cows stayed. In the stable there is a place for the donkeys and cows to lie down, and a place where they eat.

We eat meals from from plates, but donkeys and cows eat out of mangers. There was a manger in the stable where Mary and Joseph stayed.

When the baby was born, Mary had no nice cradle to put Him in. She wrapped Him up in some cloths and put Him into the manger as His cradle.

Do you know what that baby's name was? His name was Jesus. And He was and is the Son of God.

Parent Note: This story begins to establish the deity of Christ which is essential in understanding the Bible. Children readily accept this. They may ask why they cannot see Him or what He looks like or how He can live in heaven as well as in their hearts. Keep your answers simple and honest, such as: we can't see Him because He does not have a body like ours, but one time He did. He was seen by people; He ate with them and talked with them. We do not know what He looks like, and we don't know how He can be in two places at one time, but He can because the Bible tells us so. The Bible is true.

Questions

- Where did Mary and Joseph find a place to sleep?
- Why was Joseph worried?
- What usually sleeps in a stable?
- What was the baby's name?
- Who had sent Jesus to Mary?
- Since Jesus was God's own Son, why wasn't He born in a palace or at least a comfortable, clean place?

Memory Verse

"For God so loved the world that he gave his one and only Son, that whoever believes in him shall not perish but have eternal life."

John 3:16

The Shepherds Meet Jesus

Luke 2:8–16

My cousins used to have sheep. They had fenced in the yard and let the sheep eat the grass. That is how they kept the grass mowed!

In the country where Jesus was born, people used to have many sheep. The sheep stayed out in the fields to eat the grass. But since there were wolves and bears in the country, men had to stay in the fields to protect them. These men were called shepherds.

On the night Jesus was born, an angel came from heaven and spoke to some shepherds. They were frightened, I suppose because they had never seen an angel before. The angel had a very important message from God.

The angel told them, "Do not be afraid. I bring you good news of great joy that will be for all people. Today in the town of David a Savior has been born to you." The angel called Jesus the Savior.

The shepherds found Jesus in the manger, as the angel said.

Questions

- Why did shepherds have to take care of their sheep?

- On the night Jesus was born, who came to talk to the shepherds?

- What did the angel tell them?

- What did the angel call Jesus?

Memory Verse

"For God so loved the world that he gave his one and only Son, that whoever believes in him shall not perish but have eternal life."

John 3:16

Wise Men Meet Jesus

Matthew 2:1–12

Some other men came to see Jesus in Bethlehem. They were called Wise Men. These Wise Men knew a lot about the stars. They used to stay up all night sometimes, looking at the stars, trying to learn all about them.

One night when they were looking up at the sky, they saw a new star that was different from all the stars they had ever seen before. God had sent that star for the Wise Men to see, so they would know His Son was born.

As soon as they knew that Jesus was born, they wanted to see Him. But they lived far away from Bethlehem. They did not know where Bethlehem was. How would they find the way? God made the star to lead them to Bethlehem.

They followed the star to Bethlehem and found Jesus. They knelt down on the ground in front of Him and worshiped Him. Then they took out some presents and gave them to Him. Afterward they traveled home.

Questions

- Who else came to see Jesus in Bethlehem?
- Why did God send the star for the Wise Men to see?
- After they had seen the star, what did they want to do?
- What did they do when they saw Jesus?
- Where did they go afterward?
- How does God lead us to Jesus today?

Memory Verse

"For God so loved the world that he gave his one and only Son, that whoever believes in him shall not perish but have eternal life."

John 3:16

God Is Good

Psalm 100

> Shout for joy to the LORD, all the earth.
> Worship the LORD with gladness;
> come before him with joyful songs.
> Know that the LORD is God.
> It is he who made us, and we are his;
> we are his people, the sheep of his pasture.
> Enter his gates with thanksgiving
> and his courts with praise;
> give thanks to him and praise his name.
> For the LORD is good and his love endures forever;
> his faithfulness continues through all generations.

Questions

- Who made us?
- Who should we thank?
- Who will love us forever?

Memory Verse

"For God so loved the world that he gave his one and only Son, that whoever believes in him shall not perish but have eternal life."

John 3:16

step 31

A Safe Place

Matthew 1:21

Suppose you were playing ball in your yard and the ball rolled out into the street. You ran into the street after the ball and did not look to see that a car was coming. The car was coming closer to you at a fast speed and soon would hit you. It would kill you.

But suppose that just then a strong man picked you up and carried you to a safe place so that you would not be hit by the car. That man would have saved you from the car, right?

Jesus came from heaven to save us—not from a speeding car— but to save us from our sins.

Our sins are the bad things we do, like disobeying Mom and Dad or lying or being selfish. Jesus came to save us from being punished for them after we die. That is the reason we call Him our Savior.

If you ask Jesus to forgive you and live in your heart, he promises to do it. Would you like to ask Jesus into your heart?

Parent Note: If your children indicated that they understand what sin is, take advantage of their open hearts and lead them to Jesus through a simple prayer. For a parent, there is no greater joy. Children are the only things we can take to heaven!

Questions

- What did the angel call Jesus?

- What are our sins? Can you think of some things you have done that have made God unhappy?

- Did Jesus come to help us stop doing these wrong things?

- If we love Jesus and ask for forgiveness, will we be punished for these things after we die?

- How can Jesus, who died so many years ago, take the punishment for our sins, when we're alive now?

Memory Verse

"Believe in the Lord Jesus, and you will be saved."

Acts 16:31

John the Baptist

Matthew 3:1–6; John 3:35–36

Jesus' cousin's name was John the Baptist. He was a very good man. He lived in the desert. Remember I told you that a desert is a place where practically no one lives? John the Baptist lived there.

John wore a scratchy coat and ate unusual food. He did not eat meat and bread as you probably do. He ate locusts and wild honey. Locusts are insects that look like grasshoppers.

John loved and obeyed God. God told John to leave the desert to tell people about Jesus. He would teach them that Jesus was God's Son and to get ready for Him.

John went to a place near the Jordan River. Many people came to hear what he had to say. John told them that very soon they would see their Savior and that they must get ready.

How would they get ready? Should they put on their best clothes? No, that is not what John meant. The way to get ready for Jesus was to stop doing wrong things and ask God to take away their sins.

Parent Note: I introduce in this story a bit of biblical cultural background. This helps establish the Bible as a historical book with real people and real events.

Questions

- Where did John the Baptist live?
- What did he eat?
- What did God tell him to do?
- What was the name of the big river John went to?
- What did John tell the people?

Memory Verse

"Believe in the Lord Jesus, and you will be saved."

Acts 16:31

step 33

Wash Away Our Sins

Matthew 3:13–17

Some of the people who listened to John obeyed him and stopped doing bad things. But others didn't pay any attention to him. John took everyone who listened and obeyed down to the Jordan River to be baptized.

Do you know what it means to be baptized? It means that we are sorry for all the wrong things we have done and have asked Jesus to forgive us. It is a way of saying to everyone that Jesus has washed away our sins and we have asked Him to live in our hearts.

While John was baptizing all the people at the river, Jesus came and asked John to baptize Him. And so John did.

Jesus' baptism was very special. Because Jesus never did anything wrong, there was no need to wash away any sins. He asked to be baptized to show that John's preaching was right and that soon Jesus was going to truly wash away our sins by His blood.

When Jesus came up out of the water after being baptized, a wonderful thing happened. He heard a voice from heaven speaking. It was God's voice, and He said, "This is my Son, whom I love; with him I am well pleased."

At the same time, a beautiful bird flew down and rested on Jesus. It looked like a dove, but it wasn't. It was the Holy Spirit.

Parent Note: The Holy Spirit is introduced here. If your child shows interest, a discussion as to who the Holy Spirit is and what He does (we cannot see Him but He lives in us and helps us obey God) will help your child in an important but often neglected subject. If you are unclear in your own mind about the Holy Spirit, I suggest you refer to *The Holy Spirit* by Billy Graham.

Billy Graham (man on left in water) practicing full-immersion baptism.

Questions

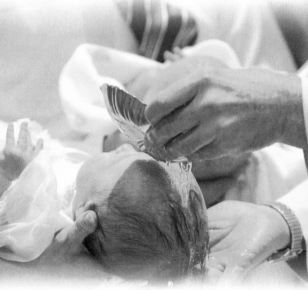

- What did John do at the river?
- What is baptism?
- Who came to John to be baptized?
- When Jesus came out of the water, whose voice did He hear?
- What did God say?

Memory Verse

"Believe in the Lord Jesus, and you will be saved."

Acts 16:31

step 34

Jesus Is Tempted

Matthew 4:1–11

The Holy Spirit led Jesus into the desert. Jesus stayed in the desert a long time—forty days and nights. He didn't have anything to eat the whole time.

While Jesus was out in the desert, Satan came to Him; he tried to get Jesus to do wrong. Remember, Satan was the one who convinced Adam and Eve to disobey God. He tries very hard to make us do wrong. He is very bad.

Satan knew that Jesus was hungry, so Satan told Jesus to change the stones lying on the ground into bread. Jesus could easily have changed the stones into bread, but He would not do it because that would be obeying Satan.

Then Satan took Jesus away from the desert to the top of a beautiful church called the temple. Satan told Jesus to throw Himself down from that high place. Satan said that God would send angels to catch Him. Then He would not be hurt when He fell.

But Jesus would not do this either, because to obey Satan would be wrong.

Then Satan took Jesus to a high mountain, and he showed Jesus many beautiful countries and cities. Jesus could see them all at the same time.

Satan told Jesus that if He would only bow down and worship him, He could have all those beautiful countries and cities for His own. But Jesus said only God should be worshiped, not Satan. In the Bible, God says that we should not worship any other gods.

When Satan realized that Jesus would not obey him, Satan went away and left Jesus. Then some good angels came and took care of Jesus.

Sometimes Satan comes to us and tries to make us do bad things. We cannot see him when he comes, but we can tell he is near, for he makes us feel like we want to do wrong.

When you feel like doing wrong things, ask Jesus to tell Satan to leave you alone. Then he will go away from us, as he went away from Jesus.

Questions

- How long did Jesus stay in the desert?

- Did He eat or drink anything?

- Who came to try to make Jesus do wrong?

- Who did Jesus say he would obey?

- What should we say to Satan when he tries to make us do wrong?

- Is temptation a sin?

Memory Verse

"Believe in the Lord Jesus, and you will be saved."

Acts 16:31

step 35

Jesus' First Miracle

John 2:1–10

Do you like to go to parties? I do—especially weddings. And I love it when they cut the wedding cake and I get a piece. I like the icing best!

Jesus liked parties, too. He went to weddings. In Jesus' day, weddings lasted up to seven days. The Bible says that Jesus and some of His disciples went to a wedding in a town named Cana.

I imagine at the wedding, there was laughter and celebrating. Maybe some dancing. A party with all kinds of good food for the guests to eat.

So many people came to this wedding that soon there was nothing left to drink.

Jesus' mother, Mary, was also at the wedding. She noticed that the wine was all gone. She was concerned and took the groom's servants to Jesus and told them, "Do whatever He tells you." Jesus told the servants to bring in some water and pour it into six tall jars in the dining room. The servants obeyed Jesus and filled the jars up to the very top.

Then Jesus told them, "Now draw some out and take it to the master of the banquet." The man tasted it and found out that it wasn't water now. It was very fine wine.

Jesus hadn't put anything into the water. He had changed the water into wine. This was His first miracle.

Jesus had authority over nature—including the jars of plain water. He could change it because He is the Son of God, and He can do the same things God can do.

Parent Note: This Scripture helps us see that Jesus wasn't always encumbered by His ministry. Here He was at a wedding party in this story. He enjoyed people and laughed. He is not stern, always demanding of us. He accepts us just the way we are. He does not hand us a list of don'ts—He gave us all things to enjoy, under authority of Scripture.

Questions

- What was the name of the town Jesus went to?
- What did Mary tell the servants to do?
- What did Jesus tell them to do?
- Who had changed the water into wine?
- Why could Jesus do miracles?
- Do you think that while Jesus was here on earth, He laughed and had fun?

Memory Verse

"Believe in the Lord Jesus, and you will be saved."

Acts 16:31

step 36

Jesus Says the Word

John 4:46–53

Jesus was in the town of Cana where He had attended the wedding party. There was a very important man who lived there. His son was very sick. He was afraid his little boy would die.

When the man heard that Jesus was in Cana, he hurried to see Him. He begged Jesus to make his son well. He told Jesus, "Sir, come down before my child dies." The man thought that Jesus would have to see his son to make him well.

But Jesus told the man, "You may go. Your son will live." The man believed what Jesus said. On his way home, his servants came out to meet the man to tell him that his son was already well.

Jesus had made the boy well by just saying so. As soon as Jesus said that, the sickness left the boy and he was well. Jesus has authority over everything, including sickness. This was a miracle!

Questions

- What did the important man ask Jesus to do?

- Could the doctors make his son well?

- What did the important man think Jesus had to do to make his son well?

- What did Jesus say to him?

- What does Jesus have authority over?

- Why didn't Jesus go to the man's house and heal the young boy there?

Memory Verse

"Come, follow me," Jesus said, "and I will make you fishers of men."

Matthew 4:19

Time Alone with God

Luke 4:42–44, 5:16

God had given Jesus a big, important job. His job was to show us what God was like and how much God loves us. Jesus knew that He had to spend time alone with God in order to do this job well.

The same is true for us. Our job is to show people what God is like. We need to spend time with God getting to know Him, reading about Him in the Bible, and talking to Him.

Early one morning before the sun was up, Jesus woke up and went out to the desert so that He could pray to God. Jesus knew how important it was to spend time alone with God.

Soon, the people from the town came to look for Jesus. When they heard that He had gone to the desert, they went out to find Him. When they found Him, they begged Him to stay in their town.

But Jesus said, "I must preach the good news of the kingdom of God to the other towns also, because that is why I was sent."

God had sent Jesus to our world to show us that God loves us. But because we have done many wrong things, called sins, we have to repent and ask God to forgive us. To repent is to be sorry for something you have done—so sorry that you never want to do it again. Jesus went to many towns telling the people these things.

Parent Note: This step introduces the doctrines of repentance and forgiveness. At this point you might want to ask your children if they want to ask Jesus to forgive them for their sins and come into their hearts.

Questions

- Where did Jesus go very early in the morning?
- Who went out to find Jesus?
- Why did God send Jesus?
- What are sins?
- What does repent mean?
- Do you follow Jesus 'example of being alone to pray?

Memory Verse

"Come, follow me," Jesus said, "and I will make you fishers of men."

Matthew 4:19

Fishermen Follow Jesus

Luke 5:1–11

Jesus came to another town named Capernaum, near the Sea of Galilee. He liked to walk on the beach.

He saw two fishing boats on the beach; they belonged to fishermen who were washing the nets.

If you ever went fishing, you probably took a fishing pole and some worms. But you could only catch one fish at a time. If you used a net, you would catch a lot of fish at a time.

Jesus told one of the fishermen, "Put out into deep water, and let down the nets for a catch."

But Peter said, "Master, we've worked hard all night and haven't caught anything. But because you say so, I will let down the nets."

Peter, James, and John rowed out on the sea. They let down their net. But when they tried to pull it back up into the boat, it was so full of fish they couldn't lift it!

The men called out to their friends to come help. They came alongside and helped pull up the net. When they emptied the fish into the boats, they were so full of fish that they were close to sinking.

This was a miracle! No one else but God could do this.

Jesus told the men to follow Him. They immediately left their boats and nets to follow Jesus.

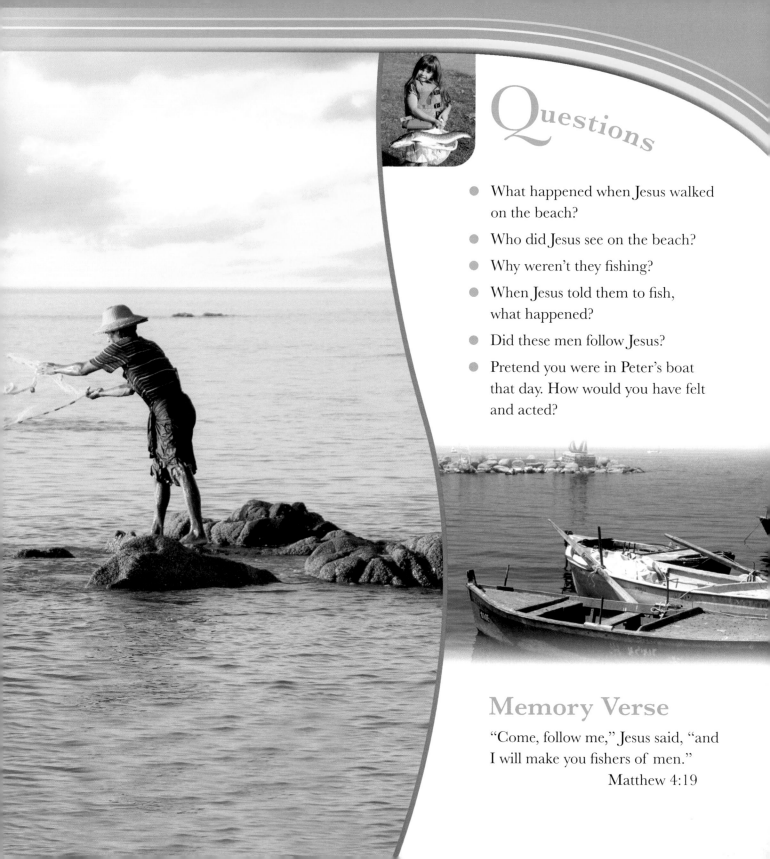

Questions

- What happened when Jesus walked on the beach?
- Who did Jesus see on the beach?
- Why weren't they fishing?
- When Jesus told them to fish, what happened?
- Did these men follow Jesus?
- Pretend you were in Peter's boat that day. How would you have felt and acted?

Memory Verse

"Come, follow me," Jesus said, "and I will make you fishers of men."
Matthew 4:19

Make Me Clean

Luke 5:12–15

A long time ago, my grandfather took me to visit a hospital where people were very, very sick with leprosy. This sickness made sores show up on a person's skin. Sometimes the sickness was so bad that people would lose feeling in their fingers or hands or feet or nose or ears.

Leprosy made people sick in the country where Jesus lived. When people got leprosy, they would have to leave their homes so that their families would not get sick. They didn't have nice hospitals to go to. They could not come back home until they were well. But no one could make them well except God.

When Jesus was walking in a town one day, a man who had leprosy came to Jesus. He knelt down on the ground in front of Jesus and said, "Lord, if you are willing, you can make me clean." Jesus didn't like to see such a sick man suffering. Jesus said, "I am willing." He then told the man, "Be clean." As soon as Jesus said that, the leprosy went away and the man was well. This was another miracle!

People couldn't help talking about how Jesus healed the man. After that, so many people came to Jesus and crowded around Him that He could not stay there anymore.

Parent Note: Leprosy shouldn't upset a child. Explain that it is not common today and medicines are available to help cure it. Emphasize the love and power of Jesus.

Questions

- What bad sickness did you learn about in this story?
- When a person got leprosy, could he stay with the family?
- Who can make a person well?
- What did the man with leprosy ask Jesus to do for him?
- Did Jesus do it?
- What did the people do?
- Why was Jesus willing to heal the man with leprosy?

Memory Verse

"Come, follow me," Jesus said, "and I will make you fishers of men."

Matthew 4:19

step 40

Rejoice and Be Glad

Matthew 5:1–12 (NIrV)

Jesus saw the crowds. So he went up on a mountainside and sat down. His disciples came to him.

Then he began to teach them. He said,

"Blessed are those who are spiritually needy. The kingdom of
heaven belongs to them.
Blessed are those who are sad. They will be comforted.
Blessed are those who are free of pride. They will be given
the earth.
Blessed are those who are hungry and thirsty for what is right.
They will be filled.
Blessed are those who show mercy. They will be shown mercy.
Blessed are those whose hearts are pure. They will see God.
Blessed are those who make peace. They will be called sons of God.
Blessed are those who suffer for doing what is right. The kingdom
of heaven belongs to them.

"Blessed are you when people make fun of you and hurt you
because of me. You are also blessed when they tell all kinds
of evil lies about you because of me. Be joyful and glad. Your
reward in heaven is great. In the same way, people hurt the
prophets who lived long ago."

Questions

- Who taught this passage to a crowd?
- Do you know someone that is like the person Jesus is describing?
- How could you become like the person Jesus is describing?
- What is our reward for believing in and following God?

Memory Verse

"Come, follow me," Jesus said, "and I will make you fishers of men."

Matthew 4:19

step 41

A Hole in the Roof

Luke 5:18–26; Mark 2:1–12

Jesus went back to Capernaum, where he had helped Peter and his brother catch so many fish. There were many houses there but they did not look like the houses you and I live in. They were small, square houses that were only one story high. The roofs on these houses were flat—a person could go up and walk around on them.

Jesus was teaching in one of these houses. In the same town, some friends of a sick man wanted to take him to Jesus, but the man was so sick and weak he could not walk.

So they decided to pick up the bed he was lying on and carry him to Jesus. When they got to the house where Jesus was, there was such a big crowd that they could not get through the door.

The man's friends carried him up onto the flat roof of the house and opened up a hole in the roof. Then they lowered the man on his bed very carefully into the room where Jesus was.

Jesus saw how much faith the men had and the effort they had to bring their sick friend to Him. He said to the sick man, "I tell you, get up, take your bed and go home." Just by saying that Jesus had made the man well. This was another miracle!

The man had been so sick that he couldn't even stand up. But now Jesus had made him well and he could walk, run, and carry his bed all the way home!

When the people who had crowded the house and doorway saw this, they were surprised and said to each other, "We have never seen anything like this!"

Questions

- When Jesus was teaching in one of these houses, who was brought to Him?
- Why couldn't the man's friends get him through the door?
- How did they get the sick man into the house?
- What did Jesus do?
- Would you go to a lot of trouble to bring a friend to Him?

Memory Verse

"Do to others as you would have them do to you…"

Luke 6:31

step 42

Read the Bible

2 Timothy 3:14–17

Every morning I get up and read my Bible. And when my grandchildren come to visit, we read the Bible together. It is important to read the Bible. It tells us about Jesus and how to live like Him.

Suppose you had done something wrong, and your father was angry and about to punish you. But your brother felt sorry for you, and asked to be punished in your place. Wouldn't that show how much your brother loved you?

This is what Jesus did for us. We have done wrong, and God was going to punish us; but Jesus loved us so much that He came down from heaven to be punished in our place. The Bible is the book that tells us about this.

Parent Note: This step underlines the substitutionary atonement of Jesus (Jesus took over our punishment for sin so that we could have a relationship with God). This is a key ingredient to the Christian faith.

the wildern...
...mportant it wa...
...e people fron...
...that He had g...
...n. When they...
...et to l...

Questions

- Who does the Bible tell us about?

- If you were going to be punished for doing something wrong, and your brother asked to be punished in your place, what would that show?

- When God was going to punish us, what did Jesus do?

- Why did He do this?

- Do you have a time each day when you read the Bible?

Memory Verse

"Do to others as you would have them do to you…"

Luke 6:31

step 43

Jesus Says to Be Kind

Matthew 6:26

Jesus walked up the side of a mountain to pray to God, His Father. Jesus prayed all night long. In the morning, twelve men had come to listen to Him. He chose these men to stay with Him all the time. They were to listen to Him and learn from Him. They were to go wherever He sent them and do whatever He said. Jesus called these twelve men *disciples.*

Jesus came down the mountain to be with a crowd of people. He was soon surrounded by people wanting to listen to Him and be healed of their diseases. Jesus taught them how to live a holy life. He told them that they should not be proud and think that they are better than other people. Instead, they must think of ways to help other people. When they realize they have done something wrong, they must be sorry for doing it.

He told the people that they must be kind to each other. I have taught my grandchildren to be kind to people, and also to all animals. I think it pleases God when we take care of His creatures.

Jesus said that the people should not fight with each other or be angry at each other. And when someone is unkind to them, they must not be unkind back. The people should be kind to them and pray for them.

Parent Note: Children have very tender hearts but can be very unkind to each other. You might point out a practical application of this story by saying, "Remember when Allison took your ball, and you hit her? What do you think Jesus would have told you to do?"

Questions

- How many men did Jesus ask to stay with Him all the time and learn from Him?

- What did Jesus tell the people on the mountain?

- How should people treat each other?

- If someone is unkind to us, what should we do?

- What are some things you can do this week to help your family or friends?

Memory Verse

"Do to others as you would have them do to you…"

Luke 6:31

The Lord's Prayer

Matthew 6:9–13

Prayer is like talking to your best friend. One day, my grandson called me on the phone. He was crying. He had lost his glasses. I prayed with him over the phone, asking Jesus to help my grandson. A few minutes after we hung up, he called back to say he found his glasses. We then thanked God for helping find his glasses.

Jesus taught the people what they should say when they were praying to God. He said, "This, then is how you should pray:

'Our Father in heaven,
hallowed be your name,
   your kingdom come,
your will be done
   on earth as it is in heaven.
Give us today our daily bread.
Forgive us our debts,
as we also have forgiven our debtors.
And lead us not into temptation,
   but deliver us from the evil one.
for yours is the kingdom and the power,
   and the glory forever. Amen.' "

This is called the Lord's Prayer, because the Lord Jesus teaches us to say it. But whenever we say this prayer, we must remember that we are speaking to God—we must think about what we are saying.

Jesus not only teaches us to say the Lord's Prayer, but He tells us to pray to God for everything we need. For God is our Father who lives in heaven, and He loves to give His children the things they pray for, and the things that are best for them.

Parent Note: Prayer cannot be overemphasized. But we can't expect our children to learn to pray if we don't pray ourselves. Children's prayers are so precious as they learn to talk to Jesus. What a privilege to teach them how! Remind them that they can pray about anything: needs, wisdom, guidance, protection, friends, sick pets, sore fingers, help in finding a lost toy—everything! As you pray with them, keep it simple and short. And don't forget to thank God for His answers.

Questions

- What did Jesus teach the people?
- What is the name of the prayer that Jesus taught them?
- When we say this prayer, to whom are we speaking?
- What should we pray to God for?
- Does God love to give to His children the things that are best for them?
- Can you think of something you prayed about and how God answered?

Memory Verse

"Do to others as you would have them do to you…"

Luke 6:31

Pray to Please God

Matthew 6:5–8

There were some men in Jesus' country called Pharisees. They were the leaders and teachers. But they thought they were better than other people. They didn't like Jesus or what He taught.

The Pharisees used to say their prayers out in the open, where people could hear them. They wanted people to think they were good—and they wanted praise from other people. Whenever anyone looked at them, they were very careful to do good things; but when no one looked at them, they weren't as concerned about what God thought of their prayers.

The Pharisees didn't want people to listen to Jesus, but to them instead. They were always trying to find something wrong with Jesus and His disciples. They were not nice.

Jesus said we shouldn't be like the Pharisees. We should not say our prayers for other people to hear, but for God to hear. We shouldn't do good things because we want other people to think we are good. We should do good things because we want to please God.

Questions

- Why did the Pharisees want people to hear them?

- When anybody was looking at them, what were the Pharisees very careful to do?

- When no one saw them, did it matter as much?

- Who do we want to hear our prayers?

- Is it easier to be good when someone is watching you?

Memory Verse

"Do to others as you would have them do to you…"

Luke 6:31

Have Faith

Matthew 8:5–13

Jesus traveled back to the town of Capernaum. A man who was a Roman commander lived there. This soldier had a servant who was very sick. The soldier was afraid that the man would die.

So the soldier said to Jesus, "Lord, my servant lies at home paralyzed and in terrible suffering." Jesus told the soldier, "I will go and heal him." But the soldier replied, "Lord, I do not deserve to have you come under my roof. But just say the word, and my servant will be healed. For I myself am a man under authority, with soldiers under me. I tell this one, 'Go' and he goes; and that one, 'Come' and he comes. I say to my servant, 'Do this' and he does it."

Jesus was happy that the soldier believed that just by saying so, Jesus could make the man well. Jesus told the soldier, "Go! It will be done just as you believed it would."

The soldier went home and found that the sickness had left his servant. He was already well, just as Jesus had said. This was a miracle.

Questions

- Who came to Jesus when He was in Capernaum?
- What was wrong with the man who worked for the soldier?
- What did the soldier want Jesus to do?
- Why was Jesus happy?
- When the soldier got home, what did he find?

Memory Verse

"Be strong and courageous ...
For the LORD your God goes with
you; he will never leave you nor
forsake you."

Deuteronomy 31:6

step 47

Back to Life

Luke 7:11–16

Jesus traveled to another town called Nain. Nain had a wall with gates so the town officials knew who was going in and out.

As Jesus came closer to the town, He met some men coming out of the gate. They were carrying a dead man in a coffin. They were going to bury him in a grave.

The dead man was his mother's only son and she was a widow. Her husband had already died, so now she lived alone. She was walking in front of the coffin. She was crying. She did not think she would ever see her son again.

When Jesus saw this woman crying, His heart went out to her. He said, "Don't cry." Then He went over to the coffin where her son lay and touched it. The men carrying the coffin stopped.

Jesus spoke to the dead man. He said, "Young man, I say to you, get up!" As soon as Jesus said these words, the dead man came to life again. He got out of the coffin, and began to talk. The man and his mother were together again!

This was a miracle.

When the people saw the dead man come to life, they were filled with wonder and praised God. They said that surely Jesus had been sent from God because no one else could bring a man back to life.

Gates of Nain

Questions

- When Jesus got close to the town of Nain, who was being carried out of the gate?

- What did Jesus say to the man's mother?

- What did He say to the dead man? What happened then?

- How did the people feel when they saw the dead man come to life?

- Who did they say had sent Jesus to them?

Memory Verse

"Be strong and courageous …
For the LORD your God goes with
you; he will never leave you nor
forsake you."

Deuteronomy 31:6

step 48

Lotion in a Jar

Luke 7:36–50

In the country where Jesus lived, people used to buy a very nice lotion called ointment. They would use the ointment to rub on their hair and skin to make them soft and smooth. The ointment smelled like flowers.

One day a man invited Jesus to his house for dinner. In that country, instead of having tables and chairs in the dining room, they had a very low table and sat on big pillows. Also, instead of shoes, the people usually wore sandals because it was very hot.

While Jesus was eating dinner at the man's house, a woman came inside where they were eating. She held a little jar of ointment. It had cost her a lot of money. She went over to Jesus, knelt at his feet, and began crying. Then she dried Jesus' feet with her hair, kissed them, and poured the ointment on them. The woman did this to show how much she loved Jesus. She loved Him because He forgave her.

Remember what a Savior is? Remember the story I told you to help you understand it? I said that suppose you were running after a ball and ran into the street. You didn't see a car coming—but a man nearby did. He ran out and pulled you out of the street just in time. That man would have saved you from being killed by the car.

In the same way, Jesus came from heaven to forgive this woman and save her from her sins. She had disobeyed God by doing many bad things, but now she was truly sorry for her sins and didn't want to do bad things anymore. Jesus told her that because she was sorry for her sins, God would forgive her and would not punish her. When Jesus did this, He was her Savior. She loved Him for coming from heaven to save her from her sins.

Questions

- What did the woman pour the ointment out of?
- What did she do to Jesus' feet?
- Was she sorry for the bad things she had done?
- When Jesus forgave her, what was He to her?
- Did she love Him because He forgave her?
- Would you give something to Jesus that cost you a lot of money?

People kept their ointment in jars made of alabaster, shown here.

Memory Verse

"Be strong and courageous …
For the LORD your God goes with you; he will never leave you nor forsake you."

Deuteronomy 31:6

step 49

Good Soil

Matthew 13:3–8; Mark 4:3–8; Luke 8:5–8

One day, Jesus told a parable to some people. A parable is a story that teaches something very important.

This parable was about a man who planted wheat in his field. Wheat grows up like tall grass and is harvested, and the little kernels of wheat are collected to grind into flour. Bread is made out of wheat flour.

The man in this parable scattered some seeds on the ground as he walked along. But some wheat fell outside the field. Birds flew down and ate the seeds.

Some of the seeds fell in the wrong place—where there were lots of rocks and no soil. The wheat could not form roots and grow up. Some seeds fell where there were lots of thorny bushes. The bushes would not give the wheat any room to grow. The wheat was crowded out.

But the rest of the seeds fell where the ground was soft and fertile. The wheat got plenty of rain and sun, so they formed roots that went deep into the ground. The plants grew tall. Soon it was harvested and the man had much more than he had at the beginning.

This same thing happens when I teach what Jesus wants people to know. Some people do not listen. It is as if birds came and took away every word I spoke, because the people do not remember.

But some people remember and they let my words about Jesus speak to their hearts.

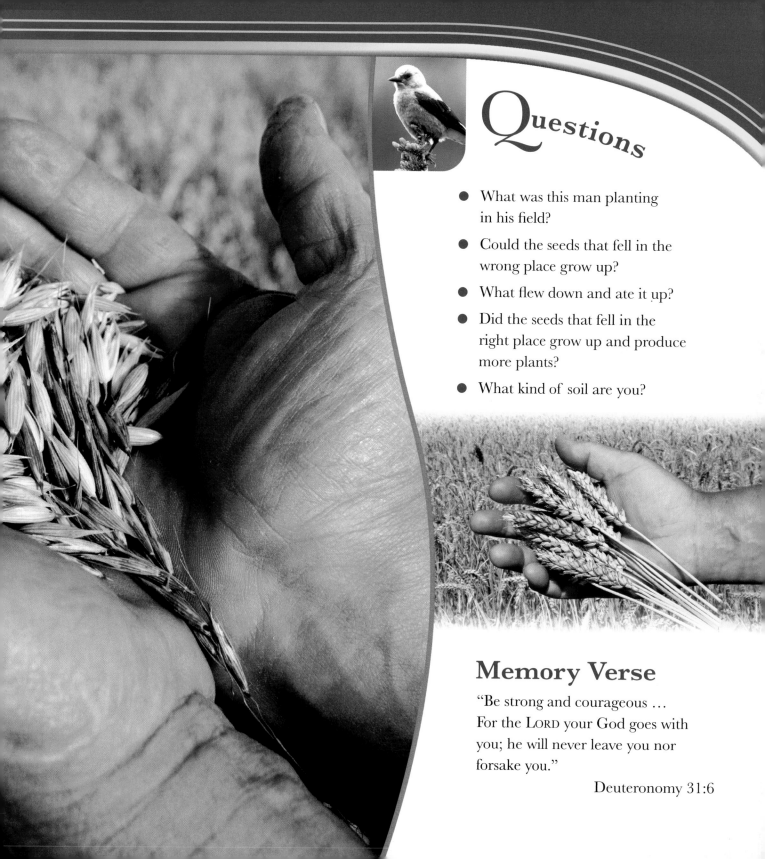

Questions

- What was this man planting in his field?

- Could the seeds that fell in the wrong place grow up?

- What flew down and ate it up?

- Did the seeds that fell in the right place grow up and produce more plants?

- What kind of soil are you?

Memory Verse

"Be strong and courageous …
For the LORD your God goes with you; he will never leave you nor forsake you."

Deuteronomy 31:6

step 50

The Fruit of the Spirit

Galatians 5:22–26

The fruit of the Spirit is love, joy, peace, patience, kindness, goodness, faithfulness, gentleness and self-control. Against such things there is no law.

Those who belong to Christ Jesus have crucified the sinful nature with its passions and desires.

Since we live by the Spirit, let us keep in step with the Spirit.

Let us not become conceited, provoking and envying each other.

Questions

- What are the fruits of the Spirit?
- What is your favorite one?
- Are any of them hard to follow or appreciate?

Memory Verse

"Be strong and courageous …
For the LORD your God goes with
you; he will never leave you nor
forsake you."

Deuteronomy 31:6

step 51

Seeds of Faith

Matthew 13:31–32

I was in my garden planting seeds one day. Some were big seeds and some were very small. They sprouted a few days later and soon I had pretty flowers.

Jesus told people about the mustard seed. It is a very small seed—about the size of a pin head. If you held one in your hand, you would hardly be able to see it. But if you planted it in the ground, it would sprout and grow into a plant big enough for birds to sit on its branches.

The words Jesus speaks to your heart are like a tiny mustard seed planted in the ground. As you water it by obeying Jesus, learning all you can about Him, and talking to Him, the seed grows bigger and bigger—like the mustard seed when it grows up to be a beautiful plant.

These are mustard plants.

Questions

- What kind of seed did Jesus tell the people about?

- How big is the mustard seed?

- When it is planted, what does it grow up to be?

Memory Verse

...It is by grace you have been saved, through faith—and this not from yourselves, it is the gift of God.

Ephesians 2:8

Bread with Yeast

Matthew 13:33

I like to make bread. The whole house smells good when it bakes in the oven. Then it tastes so delicious when I slice it and spread butter on a warm piece.

Jesus told a story about a woman making bread. First she takes some wheat flour, and then adds some salt. Then, before adding water, she adds something called yeast. She begins to mix it all together to make dough.

She works it some more with her hands—this is called kneading the dough. She kneads the dough so that the yeast will be mixed in. Then she sets the dough aside, covers it up, and leaves it for several hours. When the dough is baked later in the oven, the yeast makes nicer, softer bread.

When we keep our hearts soft to Jesus and we allow His Word to be "kneaded" in our lives, we begin to love Him more and more. And as we love Him more, we begin to live like Jesus. We actually want to obey Him and be just like Him!

Questions

- What was the woman in the story making?
- After she had mixed the flour, salt, and water, what else did she add?
- What does the yeast do?
- How is Jesus' word like the yeast?

Memory Verse

... It is by grace you have been saved, through faith—and this not from yourselves, it is the gift of God.

Ephesians 2:8

Beautiful Pearls

Matthew 13:45–46

Jesus told the people a story about a man who wanted to buy some pearls. Pearls are beautiful little round white stones created inside an oyster, which lives deep in the ocean. Sometimes we see pearls in rings or bracelets or necklaces.

The man in Jesus' story did not want to dive down under the water to find them. He wanted to buy them from the divers who had found them already. So he went to the divers and asked to see all the pearls they had to sell.

At last one of the men showed him a very beautiful pearl. It was larger and prettier than any pearl he had ever seen before, but it would cost more money than he had. So he told the diver to keep that pearl until he came back again. Then he sold everything he had so he could get enough money to buy that pearl.

Perhaps he had horses, cows, sheep, and land. He sold everything to get money to buy the pearl. When he finally had the pearl, he was very pleased because he had the thing that he wanted more than anything else in the world.

What should we want more than anything else in this world? It isn't a pearl, for that will not make us happy.

We should want to please God and ask Him to come into our heart to live. We should obey Him, learn about Him, and talk to Him. And when we do wrong, we should ask God to forgive us.

We should want this as much as the man wanted the beautiful pearl.

Questions

- What did the man in the story want?
- What did he do to get enough money to buy it?
- How did he feel when he got the pearl?
- Did he want it more than anything else?
- Should we want to please God that much?

Memory Verse

... It is by grace you have been saved, through faith—and this not from yourselves, it is the gift of God.

Ephesians 2:8

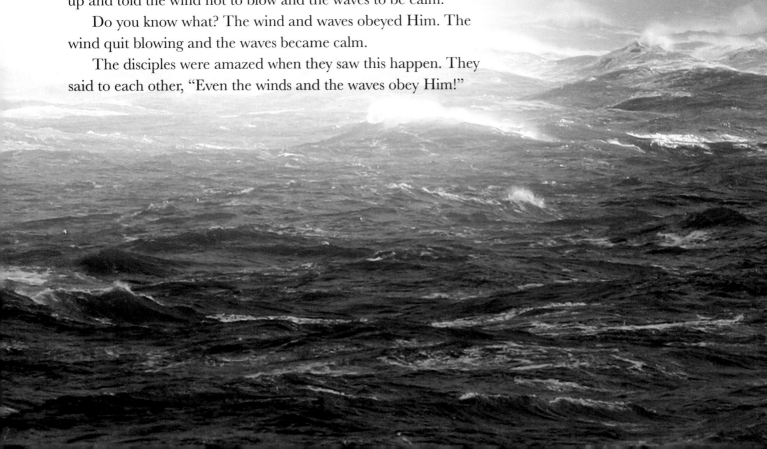

Jesus Calms the Storm

Matthew 8:23–27; Mark 4:35–41; Luke 8:22–25

Jesus got into a boat with His disciples to go across a lake. While they were sailing, He lay down and went to sleep. He was tired.

Pretty soon a storm came up that made the waves very high and rough. The little boat was being tossed around on the lake, and water was spilling into the boat. The disciples were scared. They were afraid the boat would sink.

They woke up Jesus and said, "Lord, save us, we're going to drown!"

Jesus asked the disciples why they were afraid of the wind and the waves while He was there to keep them safe. Then Jesus stood up and told the wind not to blow and the waves to be calm.

Do you know what? The wind and waves obeyed Him. The wind quit blowing and the waves became calm.

The disciples were amazed when they saw this happen. They said to each other, "Even the winds and the waves obey Him!"

Questions

- What was Jesus doing in the boat during the storm?

- How did the disciples feel? What did they do?

- What did they say to Jesus?

- Should they have been afraid while He was with them?

- If you had been in the boat that day, what would you have done?

Memory Verse

...It is by grace you have been saved, through faith—and this not from yourselves, it is the gift of God.

Ephesians 2:8

Jesus Has Power Over Demons

Mark 5:1–20; Luke 8:26–38

Remember I told you about the good angels that live in heaven? Well, there are some very bad angels that do not live in heaven. No one bad or wicked lives in heaven. We call these bad angels "demons."

Demons do not have bodies like ours with hands and feet. We cannot see demons and they can go into places where we cannot go. Sometimes demons torment people and make them very sad. Sometimes they even make people do bad things. Fortunately, Jesus is stronger than the most powerful demon.

When Jesus got out of the boat and walked on the shore, a man came to Him who was tormented by demons. The demons made this man very angry and mean so that he acted like a wild animal.

Not even chains around his hands and feet could hold him down. He would just break the chains and roam around in the mountains. All the people were afraid of him and stayed very far away.

There were caves in these mountains. Sometimes wild animals lived in the caves. This poor man with the demons lived in the caves.

Day and night, the man would cry out and cut himself with sharp rocks.

The poor man could do nothing to make the demons go away. But Jesus could make them leave. Jesus spoke to the demons and told them to come out of the man.

Nearby was a big herd of pigs that were eating. The demons asked if they could live in the pigs instead, and Jesus said, "Yes." The demons went into the pigs—then ran them into the lake where they all drowned.

The man was changed. He was not mean and angry; instead he was quiet and calm like other people. Jesus had made the demons leave the man alone. He thanked Jesus and wanted to follow Him. But Jesus told him to go home and tell his friends how he had been made well.

Parent Note: The existence of demons should not scare a child. The emphasis should be put on Jesus' power, and His love and care for us. We must not confuse mental illness with demon possession, or vice versa. They are very different. We have authority over demons by the power of Jesus' blood and name.

Questions

- Can we see demons?
- Who is more powerful—the demons or Jesus?
- When Jesus was walking on the shore, who came to Him?
- What had the demons made this man act like?
- What did Jesus make the demons do?
- Was the man well after that?

Memory Verse

...It is by grace you have been saved, through faith—and this not from yourselves, it is the gift of God.

Ephesians 2:8

step 56

One Touch: Healed

Luke 8:43–48; Matthew 9:18–26; Mark 5:24–33

A big crowd was following Jesus. Some people were very close to Him and bumping against Him.

In the crowd there was a woman who had been sick for a long time. She had gone to see many doctors, hoping they could make her well. She had spent all her money but they could not cure her.

As soon as she saw Him, she said to herself, "If I could just touch His clothes, I will be healed." So she crept up quietly behind Jesus, reached out, and touched His clothes. Immediately, she knew that she was well.

Jesus stopped and looked around. He asked who touched His clothes. The disciples had not seen the woman do it, and with so many people crowded around, they wondered why Jesus asked who had touched Him. But Jesus said, "Someone touched me; I know that power has gone out from me."

When the woman saw that Jesus knew she had touched Him and that she could not hide, she was afraid. She came to Jesus and knelt in front of Him. She told Him that she had touched His clothes and had been made well.

Jesus spoke to her very kindly. He said, "Daughter, your faith has healed you. Go in peace."

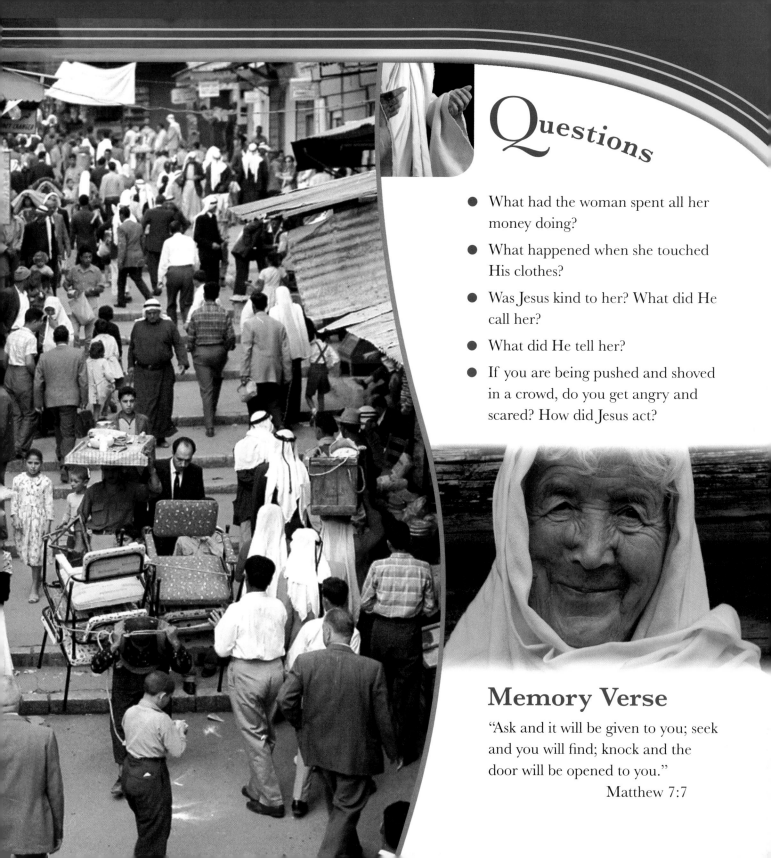

Questions

- What had the woman spent all her money doing?

- What happened when she touched His clothes?

- Was Jesus kind to her? What did He call her?

- What did He tell her?

- If you are being pushed and shoved in a crowd, do you get angry and scared? How did Jesus act?

Memory Verse

"Ask and it will be given to you; seek and you will find; knock and the door will be opened to you."

Matthew 7:7

step 57

Just Believe

Mark 5:22–24,35–42

A man came to Jesus who was very upset because his little girl was sick and he was afraid she was going to die. The man said, "Please come and put your hands on her so that she will be healed and live."

So Jesus went with the man, but as they were approaching the house, someone came to them and told the man, "Your daughter is dead; why bother the teacher any more?" But Jesus told the man, "Don't be afraid; just believe."

When they went inside the house, people were crying; they were very sad that the little girl was dead. Jesus told them to leave the house. He took three of His disciples and the little girl's parents into the room where she lay.

Jesus went to the side of her bed, held her hand, and said, "Little girl, I say to you, get up!" As soon as He said that, the little girl opened her eyes, sat up, and began to walk. She was alive again!

Jesus told her parents to get her something to eat. They were so happy because their little girl was alive. She would live with them and love them just as before.

Parent Note: When we experience difficulties or are faced with change or the unknown, we often feel afraid. Jesus does not want us to feel that way. He wants us to trust Him. The opposite of fear is faith and trust.

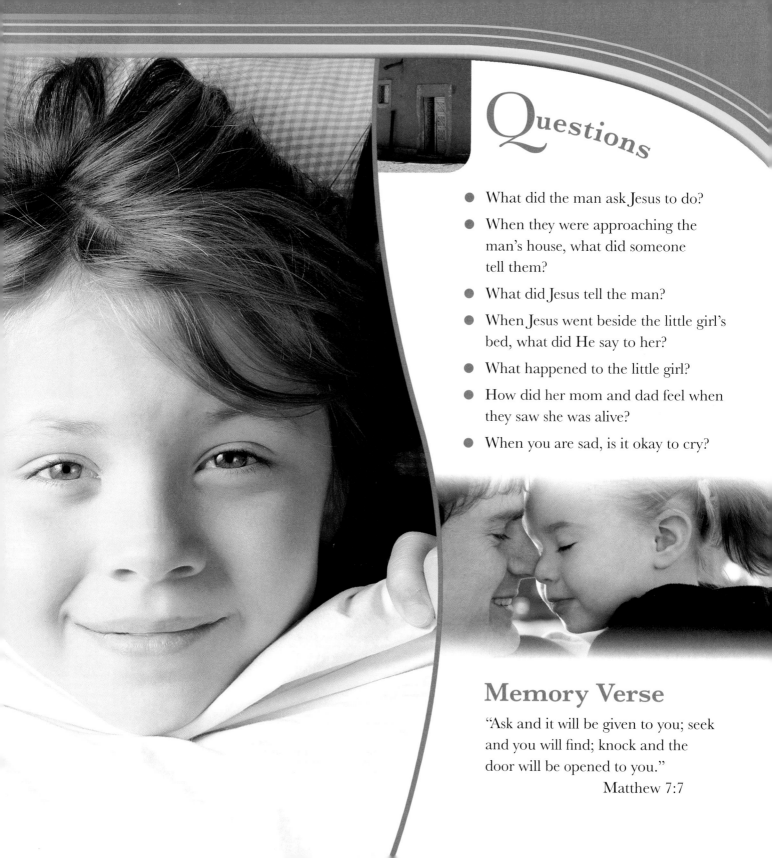

Questions

- What did the man ask Jesus to do?
- When they were approaching the man's house, what did someone tell them?
- What did Jesus tell the man?
- When Jesus went beside the little girl's bed, what did He say to her?
- What happened to the little girl?
- How did her mom and dad feel when they saw she was alive?
- When you are sad, is it okay to cry?

Memory Verse

"Ask and it will be given to you; seek and you will find; knock and the door will be opened to you."

Matthew 7:7

God Watches Over Us

Matthew 10:29–32

We learn all about Jesus and His Father, God, in the Bible. The Bible is what God wants us to know and learn about Him. One thing God wants us to know is that He loves us very much.

He doesn't say life will be easy or that He will give us everything we want. But He promised He will always watch over us.

God gives the birds food to eat. He cares about the birds. Did you know that if one tiny little bird falls out of its nest, God knows about it? But God cares a lot more about you and those who love Him than He does about the birds. He cares so much about you that He even knows how many hairs are on your head!

If we love and obey God, we don't ever need to be afraid. God promises He will always watch over us. He keeps His promises.

Questions

- Who does the Bible tell us about?
- Does God care about the birds?
- But who does God care more about?
- If we love and obey Jesus, what will God always do?
- Does God give us everything we want?

Memory Verse

"Ask and it will be given to you; seek and you will find; knock and the door will be opened to you."

Matthew 7:7

Riches in Heaven

Matthew 8:19–20

One day a man came to Jesus and told Him that he wanted to live with Him all the time. But Jesus told the man that He had no home to live in.

Jesus said that the little birds had homes—they had their nests up in the trees. And the wild animals had homes—they had caves and holes in the ground where they could go. But when Jesus was tired, He had no place to sleep. He had no home.

Jesus was even poorer than the birds and animals. But Jesus was not always poor. He used to live in heaven—He was not poor there. He had everything to make Him happy.

Why, then, did He come to this world where He would be poor and have problems? Because He loved us, and He wanted to make us God's children—then we can go to heaven after we die. If Jesus loved us so much to come from heaven for us, we ought to love Him and ask Him to live in our hearts.

Questions

- What did Jesus say about the birds and the animals?

- What was the reason Jesus had no home?

- Was Jesus always poor?

- Why did He come to this world to be poor and have problems?

- What should we do?

Memory Verse

"Ask and it will be given to you; seek and you will find; knock and the door will be opened to you."

Matthew 7:7

The Good Shepherd

Psalm 23

The LORD is my shepherd, I shall not be in want.
    He makes me lie down in green pastures,
he leads me beside quiet waters,
    he restores my soul.
He guides me in paths of righteousness
    for his name's sake.
Even though I walk
    through the valley of the shadow of death,
I will fear no evil,
    for you are with me;
your rod and your staff,
    they comfort me.

You prepare a table before me
    in the presence of my enemies.
You anoint my head with oil;
    my cup overflows.
Surely goodness and love will follow me
    all the days of my life,
and I will dwell in the house of the LORD
    forever.

Questions

- Who is the Good Shepherd?
- Are we ever really alone? Why or why not?
- Do you pray when you get scared?
- Do you feel better after you pray?

Memory Verse

"Ask and it will be given to you; seek and you will find; knock and the door will be opened to you."

Matthew 7:7

step 61

Barns of Food

Luke 12:16–21

When my children were little, I tried to teach them to save money. I had a special box for them to put money in. We also had another box for the money they gave to God.

It is wise to save money for the future. But sometimes people try to save so much money to feel safe rather than trust God for the future. Some do it so they can buy whatever they want. Some do it to feel very important.

Jesus loved to tell the people stories to teach them things. One day, He told them a story about a man who had many good things to eat and drink. The man built great big barns to store all the food for himself.

When he had put all of it away, he said to himself, "You have plenty of good things laid up for many years. Take life easy; eat, drink and be merry."

But as soon as the man said that, God spoke to him and told him, "You fool! This very night your life will be demanded from you." Then all the things that he had saved for himself would not do him any good. Instead, someone else would get it all.

Jesus told that story to teach us to not be like that man, because all the man cared about was to get rich and do what would please himself. Instead, we should always care about others and do what will make God happy.

God gives us all things to enjoy, but the important thing is not the things we have, but our relationship with God.

Parent Note: Selfishness is a very real problem in our society. Emphasize this step by pointing out a recent family incident. Perhaps one of your children has a difficult time sharing toys.

People ate these types of food and spices in biblical times.

Questions

- Why did Jesus like to tell stories?
- What did the man in this story have?
- When he had put everything away in the barns, what did he say to himself?
- But what did God say to him?
- Who should we try to make happy?

Memory Verse

"Therefore go and make disciples of all nations, baptizing them in the name of the Father and of the Son and of the Holy Spirit."

Matthew 28:19

step 62

If You Have Faith

Matthew 9:27–31

Two blind men were following Jesus one day. They could not see Him, but someone had told them that Jesus was there. Perhaps they had heard how He brought the little girl to life again, and they thought He could make their eyes well.

So the blind men followed Jesus, and called after Him, saying, "Have mercy on us, Son of David!" Jesus stopped and asked them, "Do you believe that I am able to do this?" They said, "Yes, Lord."

"According to your faith will it be done to you," He said. Then He put out His hand and touched their eyes. By only touching them, He made their eyes well. They were so happy!

They went away and told all the people who lived in that country how Jesus had cured them in one moment.

Parent Note: A blind person cannot see all the beautiful things God has made, like the sun and sky. Have you children close their eyes and imagine what it would be like to be blind.

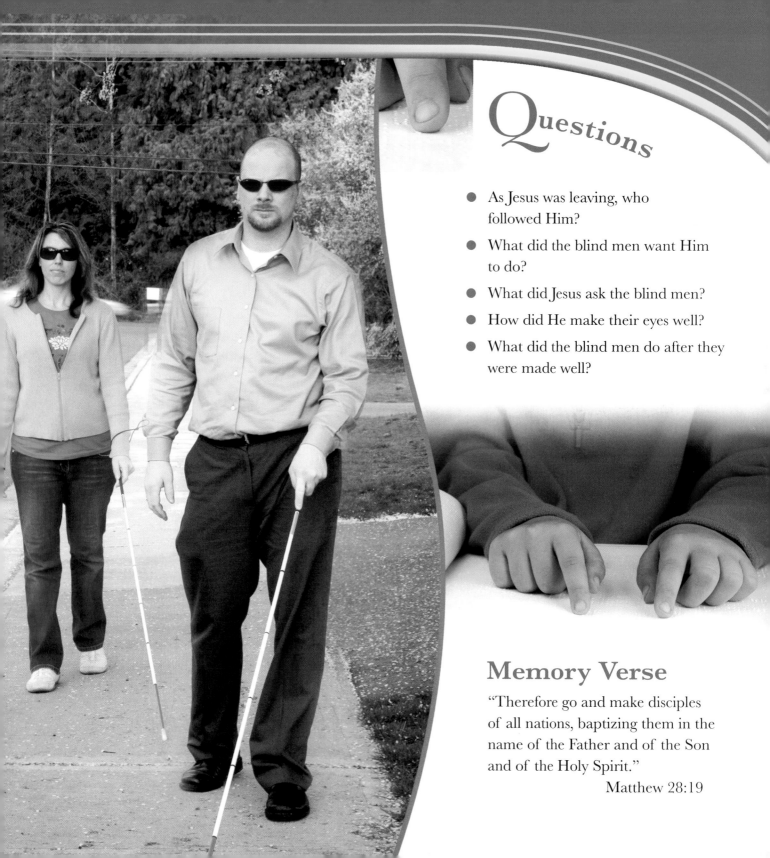

Questions

- As Jesus was leaving, who followed Him?
- What did the blind men want Him to do?
- What did Jesus ask the blind men?
- How did He make their eyes well?
- What did the blind men do after they were made well?

Memory Verse

"Therefore go and make disciples of all nations, baptizing them in the name of the Father and of the Son and of the Holy Spirit."

Matthew 28:19

step 63

Disciples Teach, Too

Mark 6:7–15

Jesus went to many other towns to teach the people. But He could not teach all the people by Himself: there were too many of them. So He sent out His twelve disciples to teach the people who lived in the cities where He could not go.

The disciples went to the towns and taught the people about Jesus. They told the people how He had come down from heaven to take away their sins and make them God's children. Jesus enabled the disciples to make sick people well and dead people alive, just as Jesus did Himself. He let the disciples do these wonderful miracles so that the people would listen to what the disciples said and believe that God had sent them.

After the disciples had taught the people, they came back to Jesus. They told Him where they had been and what they had done.

Questions

- Did Jesus go to other towns to teach people?

- Why could He not teach all the people in other cities by Himself?

- Who did He send to teach the people in the towns where He could not go?

- What did the disciples do while they were teaching the people?

- Could they have done this without Jesus' help?

Memory Verse

"Therefore go and make disciples of all nations, baptizing them in the name of the Father and of the Son and of the Holy Spirit."

Matthew 28:19

step 64

Lots of Leftovers

John 6:1–15; Mark 6:32–44

Jesus and His disciples wanted to be alone, so they got into a boat and went to the other side of the lake. But when the crowd saw where Jesus was going, they followed Him.

Jesus was kind to them; He taught them about God and heaven. He healed the sick people.

As it got dark, the disciples went to Jesus and said, "This is a remote place…and it's already very late. Send the people away so they can go to the surrounding countryside and villages and buy themselves something to eat." Jesus told the disciples, "You give them something to eat."

The disciples told Jesus that would cost a lot of money! They wanted to know if they should spend that much on bread and give it to the crowd to eat.

Jesus asked them, "How many loaves do you have?" They told Him they had only five loaves of bread and two small fish.

Jesus took the loaves of bread and fish in His hands and thanked God for the food. He divided the bread and fish into pieces, and gave them to the disciples to serve the people.

They didn't run out of food because as they gave out a piece of fish or bread, another piece would come. They had plenty. The crowd had all they wanted to eat.

After everyone was finished, Jesus told the disciples to pick up the leftovers. They had twelve baskets of food left over! This was a lot more food than when they began feeding the people.

Jesus made the bread and fish keep coming until all the people had enough to eat. This was a miracle. We cannot do miracles, but Jesus can, because He is the Son of God. He can do the same things that God can do.

Questions

- Was Jesus kind to the crowd that followed Him?

- What did Jesus tell the disciples to do?

- How many loaves of bread and fish did they have?

- Whom did Jesus thank for the food?

- How many baskets full of food were left over?

- Why could Jesus do miracles?

Memory Verse

"Therefore go and make disciples of all nations, baptizing them in the name of the Father and of the Son and of the Holy Spirit."

Matthew 28:19

Walk on Water

Matthew 14:22–33

One day, Jesus told the disciples to get into a boat and sail to the other side of the lake. He wanted to be alone, so He stayed by Himself on the beach. When the disciples left, He went up on a mountainside to pray. He knelt down on the ground and prayed to God. Remember I told you how important Jesus thought it was to spend time with God?

During the night Jesus came down from the mountainside to the beach. He saw the disciples out in the middle of the lake struggling with their boat because the wind was blowing hard against them. The waves were high and rough.

So Jesus went out to them, walking on the water. He walked on the water as if it were dry land! When the disciples saw Him coming toward them on the water, they were afraid. They did not know who or what it was.

But Jesus called out to them, "Take courage! It is I. Don't be afraid." One of the disciples named Peter asked Jesus if he could come out on the water. Jesus answered, "Come."

So Peter got out of the boat and began to walk on the water toward Jesus.

But when he heard the loud wind and saw the rough waves all around him, he got scared and began to sink. He called out to Jesus, "Lord, save me!"

Jesus reached out His hand and caught Peter so that he would not sink into the water. Jesus asked Peter why he was afraid. Jesus would take care of him and keep him safe.

As soon as Jesus and Peter got into the boat with the other disciples, the wind and waves calmed down. They were able to cross the lake.

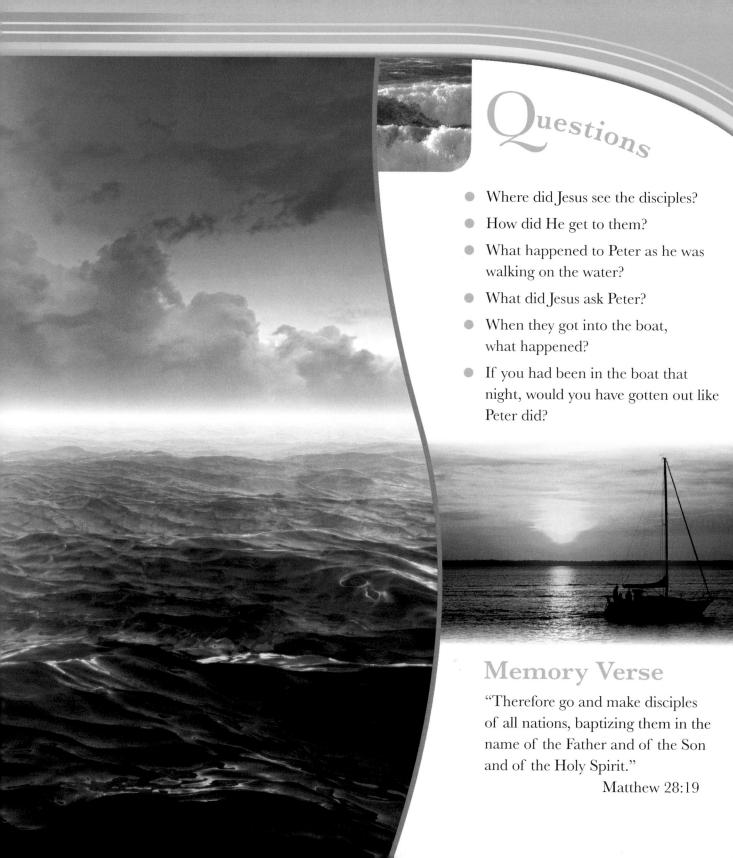

Questions

- Where did Jesus see the disciples?
- How did He get to them?
- What happened to Peter as he was walking on the water?
- What did Jesus ask Peter?
- When they got into the boat, what happened?
- If you had been in the boat that night, would you have gotten out like Peter did?

Memory Verse

"Therefore go and make disciples of all nations, baptizing them in the name of the Father and of the Son and of the Holy Spirit."

Matthew 28:19

Helping Others

Luke 9:23–26

Many people came to listen to Jesus and learn what He would teach them. Jesus told the people that if they loved Him, they would always obey Him, even if they had to do something they didn't want to do. He said, "If anyone would come after me, he must deny himself and take up his cross daily and follow me."

Suppose one day you were playing outside with some other boys and girls, but one of the boys got too rough and started to hurt one of your friends. Your friend was smaller than the others and could not play as well as they could, so the children made fun of him.

You didn't like them making fun of him and hurting his feelings, so you protected him. You made a special effort to play with him, even though the other children now wouldn't play with you.

That is taking up your cross. It is doing something that is right even though it might cause you to lose some friends or to be hurt. You do it because Jesus would have done the same thing.

Or suppose someone gave you a ten-dollar bill and told you to go buy something you wanted. You thought of a toy you wanted and your mother took you to the store to buy it.

But as you were going into the store, you saw a friend of yours who didn't have very many toys. You stopped and thought about the nice toys you had at home that this friend had admired. So you went over to him and gave him the money, and told him to go buy something he wanted. He smiled, thanked you, and hurried off to the toy section.

This is taking up the cross: putting someone else first instead of only thinking about yourself and what you want.

This makes you happy because in your heart you know you have done the right thing. But the best part is you have made Jesus happy.

Questions

- What did Jesus say people must do if they loved Him?

- What did He call this?

- If you do something right even if it may hurt you or cause you to lose friends, is this taking up the cross?

- Is thinking of other people, rather than yourself and what you want, taking up the cross?

- Does it make Jesus happy?

- Can you think of a time when you helped someone even though it caused you to lose friends?

Memory Verse

"The time has come … The kingdom of God is near. Repent and believe the good news!"

Mark 1:15

Two Visitors

Matthew 17:1–8

Jesus and three of His disciples, John, Peter and James, went up a mountain to pray. While there, Jesus' face was changed so that it looked bright and shining, like the sun. And His clothes looked as white as light.

All of a sudden two men joined them. They were Moses and Elijah, two great prophets who had lived a long time ago and now lived in heaven. They did not look like other men: They looked more beautiful.

Moses and Elijah had come back to the world where we live for only a little while to talk to Jesus.

Soon a bright cloud came onto the mountain; it covered the three disciples. They heard a voice speaking out of the cloud. It was God's voice. He said that Jesus was His Son, Who He loved very much. God told the disciples to listen to Jesus.

When the disciples heard God's voice, they were afraid. They fell face down on the ground. But Jesus told them to stand up and not be afraid.

They stood up and looked around, but the two men were not there now: They had gone back to heaven.

Questions

- What happened while Jesus was praying?

- Where do Moses and Elijah live?

- Whose voice spoke out of the cloud?

- What did God say?

- When the disciples got up from the ground, where had the two men gone?

- How does God speak to us today?

Memory Verse

"The time has come ... The kingdom of God is near. Repent and believe the good news!"

Mark 1:15

step 68

Who's the Best?

Luke 9:46–48

One day when the disciples were walking along together, they began to argue. Each of them wanted to be the greatest.

When they reached Jesus, He asked what they had been arguing about. They were ashamed and did not want to tell Him; they did not think that He had heard them. But He knows everything we say, and He knew what they had said when they were arguing.

Jesus told the disciples that they should not want to be the greatest, but they must be willing to serve other people. Jesus is not happy with us when we are proud and think we are better than other people. He is happy with us when we are humble and think of other people first instead of ourselves.

Questions

- What did the disciples argue about?
- Does Jesus know everything we say?
- When He asked the disciples why they had been arguing, how did they feel?
- What did He say?
- Does he tell us to think of other people first?
- Do you like to be first?

Memory Verse

"The time has come … The kingdom of God is near. Repent and believe the good news!"

Mark 1:15

step 69

Show Mercy

Matthew 18:23–34

One day Jesus told a parable about a king. A man who worked for the king had borrowed some money from him. Now the king wanted the money back, but the man did not have any money.

In that country, if you needed money and you had no other way of getting some, you could sell yourself, your wife, and your children to be slaves. This is what the king told the man he must do. This made the man very sad.

He begged the king to wait just a little longer so that he could find some other way to get the money. He didn't want to sell his family. He promised the king that as soon as he got the money, he would repay him.

The king felt sorry for him. The king said that the man should not sell his family to get the money. The king would forget all about the money the man owed him. The man would never have to pay back what he owed. This made the man so happy—he thanked the king for being so kind.

As the man left the king's palace, he met a man who owed him some money. He told this man to pay up. The poor man said he couldn't but promised to as soon as he could.

The man who worked for the king got very mad and demanded to be paid. He couldn't wait. Because the poor man couldn't pay him immediately, the man had him thrown into prison.

When the king heard about this, he got very angry. He sent for the man who worked for him and said, "You wicked servant…I canceled all that debt of yours because you begged me to. Shouldn't you have had mercy on your fellow servant just as I had on you?" The king had the man punished.

Jesus told this story to teach us that we must forgive others when they have said or done something unkind to us. Jesus said that we must forgive from our hearts.

Questions

- When the man could not pay the money, what did the king say must be done to him and his wife and his children?

- When the man heard this, what did he ask the king to do?

- What did the king do?

- When the man asked the king's servant to wait until he could get some money to pay him, was he willing to wait?

- What did the king say when he heard how cruel the man who worked for him had been?

Memory Verse

"The time has come … The kingdom of God is near. Repent and believe the good news!"

Mark 1:15

step 70

Wonderful Counselor

Isaiah 9:6–7

For to us a child is born,
    to us a son is given,
    and the government will be on his shoulders.
And he will be called
    Wonderful Counselor, Mighty God,
    Everlasting Father, Prince of Peace.
Of the increase of his government and peace
    there will be no end.
He will reign on David's throne
    and over his kingdom,
    establishing and upholding it
    with justice and righteousness
    from that time on and forever.
The zeal of the LORD Almighty
    will accomplish this.

Questions

- What child is going to be born?
- Can you remember what Jesus is also called?
- Why was Jesus born?

Memory Verse

"The time has come … The kingdom of God is near. Repent and believe the good news!"

Mark 1:15

The Cost of Following Jesus

Luke 9:51–56

One day while Jesus and His disciples were walking together, they came close to a small town. Many people lived in this town. Jesus sent some of His disciples into town to ask if they would let Him stop there to rest and eat.

But the people in the town were very unfriendly and unkind to Jesus. They told Him that He could not stay. Two of the disciples, James and John, got very mad at the people and wanted to punish them. They asked Jesus if they could bring down fire from heaven to burn up the houses and all the people.

Jesus was sad that the people in the town did not want Him to stop, but He was unhappy with James and John for wanting to do such a mean thing. Jesus told James and John, "The Son of Man did not come to destroy men's lives, but to save them."

He did not punish the people who were so unfriendly and unkind, but went on to another town to rest and eat.

This is a wall surrounding Jerusalem.

Questions

- What did the people say to Jesus' disciples?

- How did James and John feel?

- Was Jesus displeased that James and John wanted to do this?

- What did Jesus say that he had come to this world for?

- Instead of punishing the people, what did He do?

- Do you sometimes like to get back at someone who's been mean to you, as James and John wanted to do?

Memory Verse

Forgive as the Lord forgave you.
Colossians 3:13

The Good Samaritan

Luke 10:30–37

Jesus told the people another story. A man was walking alone on a dangerous road. All of a sudden, robbers jumped out of their hiding place and beat up the poor man. They took everything he had—food, clothes, and money. Then they left him beside the road to die.

After awhile another man came down the road. He was a priest in the temple who would tell people to be kind to each other. But he was not kind himself, so he passed the beaten man. He crossed over to the other side of the road, pretending not to see the man, and went away.

Soon another man came down the road, but he didn't help the poor man either. He kept on walking just as the priest had done and left the man on the ground.

But after these men had passed by without helping the poor man, someone else came by. He was called a Samaritan, and he was riding on a donkey. As soon as he saw the man lying beside the road, he stopped and got down to help him.

The Samaritan was very kind and gentle. He lifted the poor man and put him on the donkey; then he walked very carefully and slowly beside the donkey to be sure the man would not fall off. The Samaritan took the man to a nearby inn and stayed up all night to take care of him.

The next day when the Samaritan had to go away, he gave some money to the man who owned the inn and asked him to take care of the hurt man until he got well.

Jesus told this story to teach us to be like the good Samaritan. We should be kind to everyone we meet but especially to those who need our help. We should always be helpful whenever we can be, even when it is a lot of work.

Parent Note: Our society is very selfish; we "don't want to get involved." But this is contrary to the teaching of Jesus. Begin to instill in your child thoughtfulness and unselfishness by example. Perhaps one Thanksgiving, your family could serve a local food kitchen. Get involved in local nonprofits which provide food or services to senior citizens, children, or the homeless.

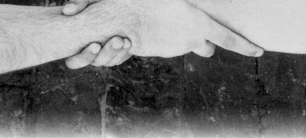

Questions

- Who beat up the man in the story and took everything that he had?

- After this happened, who first came down the road?

- Instead of helping the wounded man, what did he do?

- What did Jesus want to teach us by telling this story?

- Which man in this story are you like? Can you think of a time you helped someone who needed you?

Memory Verse

Forgive as the Lord forgave you.
Colossians 3:13

Get to Work ... or Listen?

Luke 10:38–42

Jesus visited some friends who lived in a town called Bethany. His friends were sisters named Mary and Martha. They also had a brother named Lazarus.

When Jesus came to their house, Mary stopped what she was doing to sit near Jesus to listen to what He was saying. Perhaps he was telling her about how their sins could be forgiven and how she would go to heaven when she died.

But Martha was busy in the kitchen preparing the meal. It might have been hot. She was probably tired. How could she get it all done? She had cleaned the house, and was busy trying to make her guests feel at home.

Martha asked Jesus to tell Mary to get busy and help with the housework. Jesus said, "Martha, Martha, you are worried and upset about many things, but only one thing is needed. Mary has chosen what is better." It was more important for Mary to learn what He had to say and the things He taught than to be busy doing other things.

Parent Note: Priorities are an important lesson, but perhaps more for us as parents than for children. They should be one of our priorities. Raising children is very hard work in our society. It is a huge responsibility, not to be taken lightly. In Mark 9:37, Jesus said, "Whoever welcomes one of these little children in my name welcomes me."

Questions

- When Jesus came to the house, what did Mary do?

- Why did she want to listen to Jesus?

- How did this make Martha feel?

- What did Martha ask Jesus to tell Mary?

- What did Jesus tell Martha?

- Is it easier for you to play with your toys or listen to what your parents tell you to do?

Memory Verse

Forgive as the Lord forgave you.

Colossians 3:13

Is It Really Him?

John 9:1–38

Jesus was walking along the street when He saw a man who had always been blind, even when he was a little boy. Now the man was grown up, but he couldn't work because he couldn't see.

So he would sit down in the street and beg the people who passed by to give him some money to buy food and clothes.

Jesus felt sorry for the man. He spit on the ground, stooped down, and made it into mud. He put it on the blind man's eyes. Then He told him, "Go wash in the Pool of Siloam."

The man went to the pool and washed his eyes. He could see! But it was not the mud or water in the pool that made his eyes well. Jesus made his eyes well.

When the people who knew the blind man saw him walking along like any other person who could see, they asked, "Isn't this the same man who used to sit and beg?" Some claimed that it was the man.

Others said, "No, he only looks like him." But the man himself said, "I am the man." Then they asked him, "How then were your eyes opened?" He told them, "The man they call Jesus made some mud and put it on my eyes. He told me to go to Siloam and wash. So I went and washed, and then I could see."

But the men who asked him were not happy with what he told them. They did not love Jesus and would not believe that He could make blind people well. So when the man said that it was Jesus who made him well, they were angry and would not talk to him.

Jesus heard how unkind they had been to the man. He found him and asked him, if he believed in the son of God.

"Who is he, sir?" the man asked. "Tell me so that I may believe in him."

Jesus said, "You have now seen him; in fact, he is the one speaking with you."

Then the man said, "Lord, I believe," and he worshiped Him.

This is the Pool of Siloam

Questions

- When the man had washed his eyes in the pool, what happened?

- Who made his eyes well?

- How did the people treat the man when he told them Jesus cured him?

- When Jesus told the man that God's Son had made him well, what did the man do?

- Do you have friends who don't think Jesus can help them?

Memory Verse

Forgive as the Lord forgave you.

Colossians 3:13

The Lost Sheep

Luke 15:3–7

Have you ever lost something important to you? Maybe your favorite stuffed animal. You looked everywhere for it. In the closet. Under the bed. In the car. Behind the sofa. Outside. You asked your friends and family to help you look. You looked and looked until you found it.

Jesus told a story about a shepherd who had one hundred sheep. One day when he counted his sheep, he found that there was one missing. There were only ninety-nine. The sheep was important to him, so he wanted to find the sheep and bring it back. He went to go look for the lost sheep.

Maybe like you he looked everywhere he could think of where a sheep might get lost: behind bushes and rocks. Up on a mountain. Down in a valley. Maybe he even looked in a dark, scary cave! The sheep was nowhere to be found! But he didn't give up.

He kept looking until—finally—he found the one sheep. He was so happy to finally find it! He tenderly picked up his wooly friend, put it on his shoulders and took it back home.

The shepherd called his friends and neighbors and told them he had found his sheep. "Rejoice with me; I have found my lost sheep."

When Jesus told this story, he said that when one person repents there is a party in heaven! Each person who repents is very important to Him. He said, "There will be more rejoicing in heaven over one sinner who repents than over ninety-nine righteous persons who do not need to repent."

Questions

- How many sheep did the shepherd have?
- Why did he look for the sheep?
- What did he do when he found it?
- When someone repents, what happens in heaven?

Memory Verse

Forgive as the Lord forgave you.

Colossians 3:13

step 76

The Lost Son

Luke 15:11–32

Jesus told the people a story about a man who had a son. One day the son said to his father, "Give me my share of the estate." He said that he wanted it right away. So his father gave him all the money set aside for him.

The son took the money and left his father's house. He went far away to another country. He wasted all the money his father had given him until it was all gone.

So he had to go to work just to get something to eat. The man he worked for sent him out to feed the pigs but never gave this young man enough to eat. He got very hungry.

He began to think about his father's house. No one was hungry, not even the people who worked for his father. He always had plenty to eat, a bed to sleep in, clean clothes, and a father who loved and cared for him. So he said to himself, "I will set out and go back to my father and say to him, 'Father, I have sinned against heaven and against you. I am no longer worthy to be called your son; make me like one of your hired men.' Perhaps he will forgive me and let me work for him."

So he headed home. When he was still far away, his father saw him. His father did not wait for him to come any closer, but ran down the road to meet him. His father was so happy! He gave his son a big hug and kiss.

The son began to tell his father how sorry he was to have been so selfish and greedy to take the money and leave home. But his father told the people who worked for him to go get new clothes for his son to wear and put a ring on his finger and shoes on his feet.

His father told them to prepare a big meal to celebrate. "I thought he was lost but now he is found," said the father.

Jesus told this story to teach us something. If we have sinned but are sorry for it, we can go to our Heavenly Father to tell Him we are sorry. He will always forgive us, just as the father in this story forgave his son.

Questions

- What did the younger son in the story ask his father to give him?

- After he had gone away and spent all the money, what did he have to do to get food to eat?

- What did the son begin to think about?

- When he was still far down the road, who saw him?

- What did his father do when the son said that he was sorry?

- Will our Heavenly Father forgive us when we tell Him we are sorry when we have sinned?

Memory Verse

"For the Son of Man came to seek and save what was lost."

Luke 19:10

Calling All Angels

Luke 16:19–28

Jesus told the people about a rich man who had a lot of money and could buy everything he wanted. He wore beautiful clothes and had good things to eat every day. In the same city where the rich man lived, there was a poor man. His name was Lazarus.

Lazarus was not only poor, he was also sick and weak—his body was covered with sores. Because he was so poor and sick, his friends used to carry him to the rich man's house and lay him down just outside the gate, so that he might be able to get the pieces of leftover bread from the rich man's dinner.

The dogs that roamed the street seemed to pity Lazarus because they came to lick his sores.

Finally, Lazarus died. God sent some of His angels to get him.

The angels came and carried Lazarus up to heaven. He was not sick or poor anymore when he got to heaven, for God loved him and made him well. He had a new body. God gave him everything to make him happy.

After awhile, the rich man died, too. But the angels did not come for him. He went to the place where wicked people go, called hell. Hell is a place where God is not. And while the rich man was being punished for his sins, he could see Lazarus far away in heaven.

The rich man wanted to go to heaven where Lazarus was, but he could not. He had done many bad things and had not asked God to forgive him. We can ask God to forgive our sins because Jesus paid for them. We can ask Him to teach us how to love and obey Jesus. Then when we die, God will send His angels to take us up to heaven, too.

Parent Note: This chapter mentions hell. Children can understand this concept because they have to deal almost daily with being punished for doing something wrong! But again, you need not dwell on the idea of punishment and hell but instead emphasize heaven and the anticipation of it if we have Jesus in our hearts.

Questions

- When Lazarus died, who carried him to heaven?

- Was he sick and poor in heaven?

- Where was the rich man sent?

- Why couldn't the rich man go to be with Lazarus in heaven?

- If we ask God to forgive us and ask Jesus to live in our hearts, where will we go when we die?

- Have you ever not helped someone because you thought you were too good?

Memory Verse

"For the Son of Man came to seek and save what was lost."

Luke 19:10

step 78

Being Sorry

Luke 17:3–5

Sometimes people would rather do bad things; sometimes it seems easier and more fun than doing what is right. But Jesus said we should not do what is wrong—like telling lies, taking things that don't belong to us, fighting with brothers or sisters, or talking back to Mom or Dad. If we are doing these things, we must stop doing them. If we ask Jesus to help us stop doing wrong, He promises to help us.

We should obey God and do what is right—that makes God happy. He won't stop loving us for doing bad things, but there will be consequences.

Perhaps someone hurts you and you get very angry. Jesus said, "If he sins against you seven times in a day, and seven times comes back to you and says 'I repent,' forgive him." If he is unkind many times, but later says he is sorry, we must forgive him every time—no matter how often it may be.

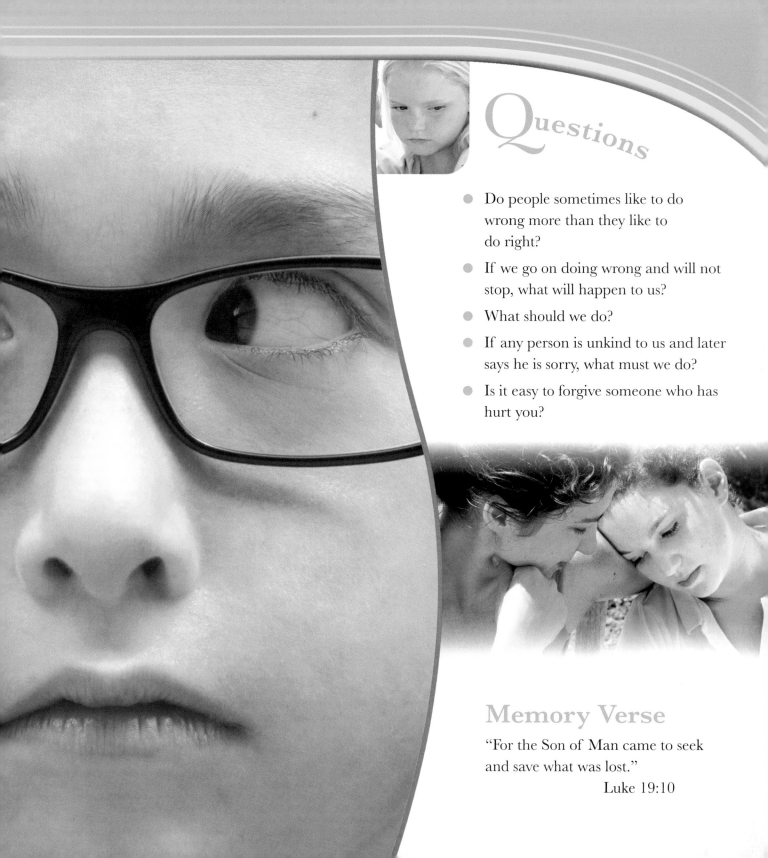

Questions

- Do people sometimes like to do wrong more than they like to do right?

- If we go on doing wrong and will not stop, what will happen to us?

- What should we do?

- If any person is unkind to us and later says he is sorry, what must we do?

- Is it easy to forgive someone who has hurt you?

Memory Verse

"For the Son of Man came to seek and save what was lost."

Luke 19:10

He's Alive!

John 11:1–6, 17–44

One day, Lazarus, a good friend of Jesus, got very sick. This was a different Lazarus than the one Jesus described who died and went to heaven. Mary and Martha sent someone to tell Jesus that their brother Lazarus was sick.

When Jesus heard, He went to their house because He loved them very much. By the time Jesus got there, Lazarus was already dead and had been buried. The people who were with Mary and Martha were so sad that Lazarus was dead. When Martha heard that Jesus was coming, she went to meet him. Mary stayed home.

Martha told Jesus that if He had been here, her brother would not have died. But she knew God would give Jesus whatever He asked.

Jesus said that her brother would rise again. "I am the resurrection and the life," He said. People who believe in Jesus would live even though their bodies die.

Jesus asked them where they had buried Lazarus. It was a cave with a big stone rolled over the front of the opening. Jesus told the people to roll the stone out of the way.

In a loud voice, Jesus said, "Lazarus, come out!" As soon as He said that, Lazarus came out! He was alive! Jesus had made Lazarus alive again by just saying those words. Jesus did this miracle so that people would honor God.

Jesus told the people nearby to undo the clothes that had been tightly wrapped around Lazarus for burial so that he could walk. Then Lazarus went home with his sisters, Mary and Martha. They were very happy.

Parent Note: Death is a matter to be discussed with children. It is more frightening to children to be uncertain about such a subject than to learn about it. But here the emphasis always should be not on death but on the promise of a wonderful heavenly home with Jesus if we have asked Him into our hearts. No doubt a member of the family—perhaps a great-grandparent or grandparent—has died during your child's lifetime. I know that in our case, while there were sorrow and tears because of our loss, there was great joy knowing the loved one was in heaven with Jesus. We would see them again one day.

Questions

- When Lazarus got sick, did they send someone to tell Jesus?
- What had already happened when Jesus arrived?
- Where had they buried him?
- When they had taken the stone out of the way, what did Jesus say?
- Who made Lazarus come back to life?

Memory Verse

"For the Son of Man came to seek and save what was lost."

Luke 19:10

Secure in Jesus Christ

Romans 8:35–39

Who shall separate us from the love of Christ? Shall trouble or hardship or persecution or famine or nakedness or danger or sword?

…In all these things we are more than conquerors through him who loved us.

For I am convinced that neither death nor life, neither angels nor demons, neither the present nor the future, nor any powers, neither height nor depth, nor anything else in all creation, will be able to separate us from the love of God that is in Christ Jesus our Lord.

Questions

- Can you think of anything that can separate you from God's love?

- What is the one thing that separates us from God?

Memory Verse

"For the Son of Man came to seek and save what was lost."

Luke 19:10

step 81

Jesus Loves Children

Matthew 19:13–15; Mark 10:13–16; Luke 18:15–17

Jesus was very busy. Many people were crowding around Him. They wanted Him to help them with their problems.

Some people brought children to Jesus. They wanted Him to hug and pray for them. But Jesus' disciples thought this would bother Him. They told the people to take the children away.

This made Jesus unhappy because He loved children (and still does!). I imagine He liked to play games with them, tickle them, and laugh with them.

He told the disciples, "Let the children come to me, and do not hinder them, for the kingdom of God belongs to such as these." He gathered them to Him, and blessed them.

Jesus loves children. If they love Him and ask Him to live in their hearts, He will always be with them.

Questions

- Who were brought to Jesus?
- Why did the disciples try to send the children away?
- What did Jesus tell the disciples?
- If children love Jesus and ask Him to live in their hearts, what will He do?

Memory Verse

"What is impossible with men is possible with God."

Luke 18:27

step 82

Big Wooden Cross

Matthew 20:17–19; Mark 10:32–34; Luke 18:31–33

Jesus told His disciples that people were going to betray and kill Him when they went to Jerusalem. (This was predicted years before by prophets.) The soldiers were going to be very cruel to Jesus. They would beat Him, call Him names, spit on Him—and then kill Him. But He told the disciples that He would be brought back to life again!

The way that Jesus would be killed would be very painful and cruel. He was going to be nailed to a cross. A cross was made of two large pieces of wood fastened together. The Roman soldiers were going to put Jesus on the cross by pounding big nails through His hands and feet into the wood of the cross. They would leave Him there until He died.

Many people in Jerusalem wanted this to happen. They were angry that He told them about their sins and for saying that He was God's Son. They did not want to be told about their sins, and they did not believe that Jesus was God's only Son.

Questions

- How did Jesus say the people would treat Him when He came to Jerusalem?

- What would they nail Him to?

- What was a cross made of?

- Why were the people so angry at Jesus?

- Would they believe that Jesus was God's Son?

Memory Verse

"What is impossible with men is possible with God."

Luke 18:27

step 83

Short Man

Luke 19:1–10

Our government is very large and does many things for people. But to do those things it needs money. Adults pay the government some money out of what they earn at work. This is called a tax.

Long ago, a king would send out men called tax collectors to get the taxes from the people. One of these tax collectors was named Zacchaeus.

When Jesus came to his town, Zacchaeus tried very hard to see Jesus. Zacchaeus was a short man and couldn't see over the heads of the other people. So he ran ahead of the crowd and climbed a tree.

When Jesus reached the tree, He looked up and said, "Zacchaeus, come down immediately. I must stay at your house today." Zacchaeus hurried down from the tree. He was very glad that Jesus was coming to his house.

Zacchaeus listened to all the things Jesus told him. He promised to do all the things Jesus told him to do. He said, "Look, Lord! Here and now I give half of my possessions to the poor, and if I have cheated anybody out of anything, I will pay back four times that amount."

This made Jesus happy. He told Zacchaeus, "Today salvation has come to this house … For the Son of Man came to seek and to save what was lost."

Jesus wants us to be kind to other people and help them when we can. He wants us to be very careful never to take anything that belongs to another person. If we have, we must give it back. This makes Jesus happy.

Questions

- Why couldn't Zacchaeus see Jesus?
- Where did he go so he could see Jesus?
- When Jesus came to the tree, what did He say to Zacchaeus?
- What did Zacchaeus say he would do?
- What can we do to make Jesus happy?

Memory Verse

"What is impossible with men is possible with God."

Luke 18:27

step 84

Hosanna in the Highest

Matthew 21:1–17; Mark 11:1–11; Luke 19:28–40

Before Jesus reached Jerusalem, He told two disciples to go to a nearby town. They would find a donkey and her young colt tied there. Jesus told the disciples to untie the animals and bring them to Him.

If anyone asked what they were doing, they would say that Jesus needed them. Then, Jesus said, the people would send the donkey and colt to Jesus.

So the disciples did what Jesus told them to do. They went to the town and found the donkey and colt. As they untied the animals, some men asked what they were doing. The disciples said that Jesus needed the animals. Then the men let the disciples take the animals to Jesus.

Jesus rode into Jerusalem on the colt's back. A big crowd of people followed Him. They all cried out,

"Hosanna to the Son of David!"

"Blessed is he who comes in the name of the Lord!"

"Hosanna in the highest!"

Some people took off their coats and laid them on the ground. Other people cut off branches from the trees and laid them on the ground for Jesus to ride over them. That was what they used to do when a king rode through the streets.

They did this to show how glad they were to have Jesus come into their city.

Then Jesus went up to the Temple. Some blind people came to Him. People who couldn't walk were brought to Him. Jesus healed them.

Questions

- What did Jesus send two of His disciples into town to find?
- What did some of the people put down on the ground for Him to ride over?
- Why did they do this?
- Who did Jesus heal?

Memory Verse

"What is impossible with men is possible with God."

Luke 18:27

step 85

Time-out

Luke 19:45–47

When Mom or Dad says you have done a bad thing, how do you feel about them? Do you get mad at them? Do you want them to go away? It is hard to have someone tell us we are wrong. It hurts us. And you might get a time-out or grounded for doing wrong. But learning when we're wrong is for our own good, to make us better people.

Jesus tried to tell some people they were doing wrong, too.

After Jesus was praised in the streets of Jerusalem, He found some people selling cattle and doves in the temple. He got very angry because this was against God's rules. He told the people to stop.

He told them about their sins. Remember I told you what sins are—they are all the bad things we do, like disobeying our parents or telling lies. In this story, people were making lots of money in the temple—where they were only supposed to pray and worship God.

The people who didn't love Jesus were getting more and more unhappy with Him. They did not want to be told about their sins. In fact, they wanted to get rid of Jesus. They wanted to kill Him.

But they were foolish to think they could try to stop God's plan.

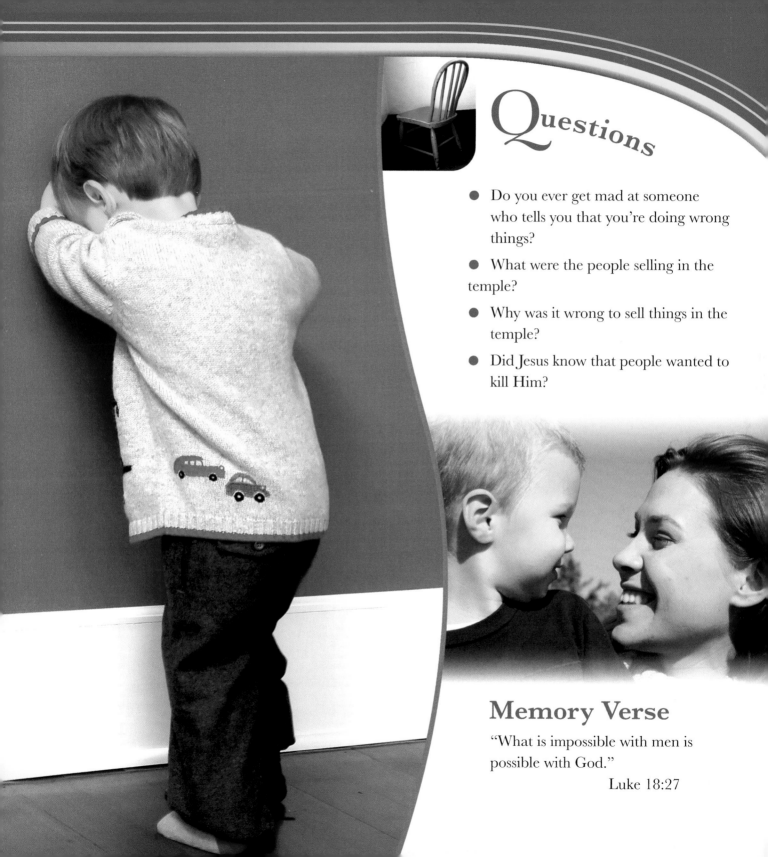

Questions

- Do you ever get mad at someone who tells you that you're doing wrong things?

- What were the people selling in the temple?

- Why was it wrong to sell things in the temple?

- Did Jesus know that people wanted to kill Him?

Memory Verse

"What is impossible with men is possible with God."

Luke 18:27

A Wedding Feast

Matthew 22:1–13

Jesus told some people a story. It was about a king who decided to have a big party because his son was getting married. When the party was ready, the king sent his servants out to say that it was time to come. But no one would come.

Then the king sent his servants out again to tell the people that it was time to come to the party. Good food was waiting on the table. But some people would not listen to the servants. And others listened but did not obey.

When the king heard what they had done, he was very angry and sent his soldiers out to punish them.

The king then called more servants and told them that although the party was ready, no one was there to eat the food. The people who had been asked to come would not be allowed to come now, since they had refused. It was too late for them.

So the king sent his servants out into the streets and found people who would come to the feast. The servants brought many people.

When the king came into the room to welcome the people, he saw a man who was not wearing wedding clothes. He asked the man why he came to the feast without them.

But the man did not know what to say to the king. The king was angry, and he told his servants to take the man out of the party. They were going to punish him.

God has given us many good things. He has prepared heaven for us and has given us everything we need to enjoy it. Asking Jesus into our hearts is the only way to go to heaven.

Questions

- When the king sent his servants to tell the people to come to his feast, what did the people do?

- Did the people who came in from the streets have nice enough clothes to come into the king's house?

- What do we have to do to go to heaven?

Memory Verse

Come near to God and he will come near to you.

James 4:8

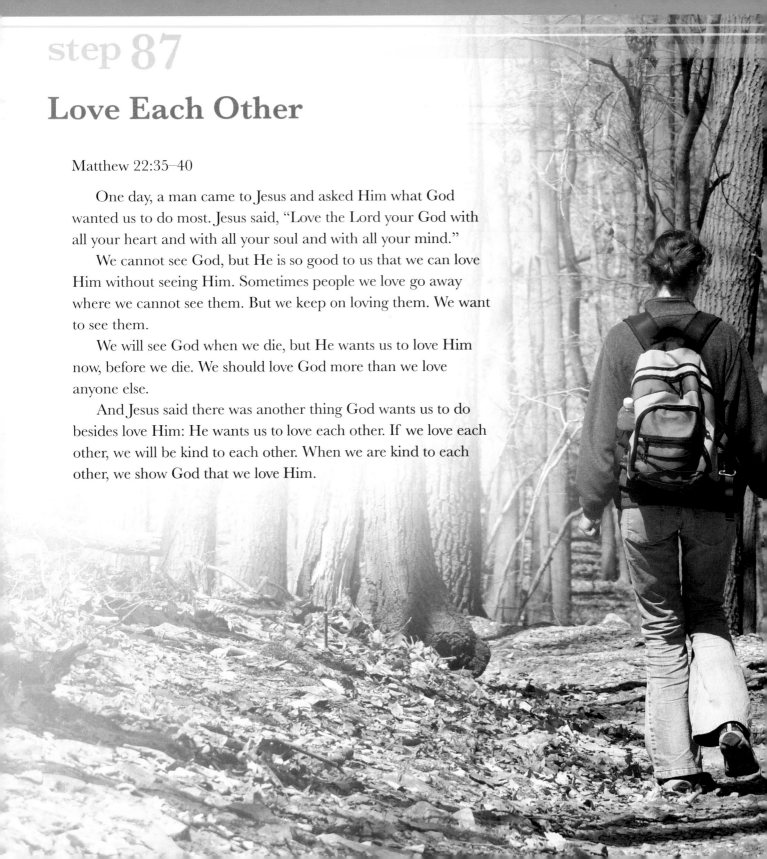

Love Each Other

Matthew 22:35–40

One day, a man came to Jesus and asked Him what God wanted us to do most. Jesus said, "Love the Lord your God with all your heart and with all your soul and with all your mind."

We cannot see God, but He is so good to us that we can love Him without seeing Him. Sometimes people we love go away where we cannot see them. But we keep on loving them. We want to see them.

We will see God when we die, but He wants us to love Him now, before we die. We should love God more than we love anyone else.

And Jesus said there was another thing God wants us to do besides love Him: He wants us to love each other. If we love each other, we will be kind to each other. When we are kind to each other, we show God that we love Him.

Questions

- What does God want us to do more than anything else?

- Who else does God want us to love besides Him?

- If we love each other, how will we treat each other?

- Why does God want us to love each other?

Memory Verse

Come near to God and he will come near to you.

James 4:8

Give God the Best

Mark 12:41–44; Luke 21:1–4

During church service, an offering plate is passed. We give money to God through the offering.

In Jesus' time the church, or temple, had a box. People dropped in just as much as they wanted to. After a lot had been dropped in, the priests opened the box and took the money out. They bought things with it for the temple. This money was the same as if it were given to God; it was God's money.

One day Jesus watched people drop their money into the box. Rich people dropped in a lot. Soon, a poor woman dropped in only a little bit of money.

Jesus said to the disciples, "I tell you the truth, this poor [woman] has put in more than all the others. All these people gave their gifts out of their wealth; but she out of her poverty put in all she had to live on."

The rich people had plenty of money left over for themselves. But the poor woman had nothing left for herself, because she gave all that she had. This showed how much she loved God.

God isn't impressed by how much we give. What matters most is that we love Him by giving Him the best that we have.

Parent Note: Giving is an important concept in the Christian faith. It should be taught early and made a lifelong habit—to give back a portion of what God has so bountifully given to us. Help your children see that it is a joy to give to God.

Questions

- Who gave the large amount of money to the temple?

- Who came and dropped in a little bit of money?

- Did the poor woman have any left for herself?

- How can we show God that we love Him?

Memory Verse

Come near to God and he will come near to you.

James 4:8

step 89

The Second Coming

Matthew 24:36–46; 1 Corinthians 15:52; 1 Thessalonians 4:16–18

Jesus told the disciples about when He was going to come back to earth again. This is called the Second Coming. The Second Coming will happen in the last days in history. Jesus will come from heaven on that day, and all the angels will come with Him. Everyone will be able to see Him.

No one knows when Jesus will come back. It could happen while you're at school or while you're sleeping. Jesus will come back when many people don't care about Him. And we know it will happen when we least expect it. That's why it's important to always be ready.

Don't wait to give your heart to Jesus or to share Him with your friends. He could come back next week or tomorrow—or even today. That's why it's best to be ready for Jesus to return.

Questions

- Who is coming to this world at the Second Coming?
- Who will come with Jesus?
- When will Jesus come back?
- Who can you tell about Jesus?

Memory Verse

Come near to God and he will come near to you.

James 4:8

step 90

The First Communion

Luke 22:19–20

…[Jesus] took bread, gave thanks and broke it, and gave it to [the disciples], saying, "This is my body given for you; do this in remembrance of me."

In the same way, after the supper he took the cup, saying, "This cup is the new covenant in my blood, which is poured out for you…"

Questions

- Who gave thanks and broke bread?
- Who did Jesus give the bread to?
- What is another word for *covenant*?
  (Hint: think Noah's rainbow)

Memory Verse

Come near to God and he will come near to you.

James 4:8

step 91

Be Prepared

Matthew 25:1–13

Jesus told a story about some young women who went out in the night, carrying lamps with them. They went out to meet a man who had just been married. This man was called a bridegroom.

When the women reached the bridegroom's house, they sat down to wait until he came home. Soon they all fell asleep.

In the middle of the night somebody called out, "The bridegroom is coming; go out to meet him." They all got up quickly and began to get ready. But they found that while they were asleep their lamps had run low on oil.

Some of the young women were wise and had brought extra oil with them; they poured this oil into their lamps so the flame wouldn't go out. These women were ready when the bridegroom came home. He invited them into his house and gave them a feast.

But the other women were foolish. They did not bring any extra oil with them, so they had to go buy some. By the time they came back, it was too late. The bridegroom had gone inside and shut the door. They could not get in.

This is the way it will be when Jesus comes again. Some people will be ready like the wise young women who had their lamps burning. And Jesus will take those who are ready up to heaven. He said, "Therefore keep watch, because you do not know the day or the hour."

But some people, like the foolish young women whose lamps were low on oil, will not be ready. If we want to be ready for Jesus when He comes back, we must love Him and ask Him to be our Savior.

Questions

- Were the wise young women ready when the bridegroom came?

- What did the foolish young women have to do?

- Where will Jesus take the people who are ready to meet Him when He comes back?

- If we want to be ready when Jesus comes back, what must we do?

Memory Verse

Now faith is being sure of what we hope for and certain of what we do not see.

Hebrews 11:1

Money Hungry

Matthew 26:14–16; Mark 14:10–11; Luke 22:3–6

The disciples followed Jesus wherever He went, and listened to what He taught. All the disciples loved Jesus—except one. Judas loved money more than anything else. He did not love Jesus.

Remember the people who wanted to kill Jesus? Judas went to these men and asked how much money they would give him if he showed them where Jesus was. The men told Judas they would pay him thirty pieces of silver.

Judas decided that as soon as he could find Jesus in a place by Himself, he would show these wicked men where Jesus was. Then they could take Jesus away to kill Him.

Questions

- Did the disciples all love Jesus?
- Which one didn't love Jesus?
- What did Judas love more than anything else?
- How much money did the men promise to give Judas?
- What did Judas decide to do?

Memory Verse

Now faith is being sure of what we hope for and certain of what we do not see.

Hebrews 11:1

The Last Supper

Matthew 26:17–46; Mark 14:12–42; Luke 22:7–46; John 14:2–3

The people who lived in Jesus' country used to have a feast for a special reason. They had this feast once a year; in fact, Jewish people still have this feast. It is called the feast of the Passover.

Jesus and His disciples wanted to eat a feast of the Passover together. But they did not have a place to have the feast. Jesus told the disciples to go into town and ask where they could hold their feast.

The disciples did exactly what Jesus told them to do. A man showed them a room to use. So the disciples prepared the feast.

That evening around suppertime, Jesus told the disciples this would be the last time He would eat the Passover feast with them. He knew that He would die soon.

Jesus told the disciples that He was going to get heaven ready for them. Later He would come back to take them to Heaven. Jesus meant that He would come back and get all the people who love Him when He comes at the Second Coming.

After they had eaten, they sang a song together. Then they went to a garden. Jesus went off by Himself to pray.

Jesus knew that some men were going to take Him that night and kill Him. He told God, "My Father, if it is possible, may this cup be taken from me. Yet not as I will, but as you will." He didn't want to die, but He knew that was the only way we could have our sins forgiven and go to heaven.

Questions

- What was the name of the feast that was celebrated by Jesus and His disciples?

- What did Jesus tell the disciples as they were eating?

- Is Jesus going to come back and take all those who love Him to heaven?

- What did Jesus do in the garden?

- Why was Jesus willing to die?

- What kind of place do you think heaven will be?

Memory Verse

Now faith is being sure of what we hope for and certain of what we do not see.

Hebrews 11:1

Betrayed

Matthew 26:47–50

After the Passover feast, Jesus went to the garden to pray. Most of the disciples went with Him.

Judas, the disciple who didn't love Jesus, did not go to the garden with Jesus. Instead, he found the men who wanted Jesus killed and told them where Jesus was.

The men paid Judas thirty pieces of silver they had promised him.

Some men went with Judas to get Jesus. The men carried sticks and swords to fight with. They carried lanterns, too, so they could see in the dark. Judas showed the way to the garden.

On the way, Judas told them how they would know which one was Jesus. Judas would go up to Jesus and kiss Him.

Soon they reached the garden. Judas went up to Jesus and said, "Greetings, Rabbi," and kissed Him. The men grabbed Jesus and took Him away.

This is the Garden of Gesthemane, where then men found Jesus.

Questions

- Did Judas go with Jesus to the garden?

- Who did Judas tell where Jesus had gone?

- What did those men give Judas?

- How did Judas say they would know which one was Jesus?

- After Judas had kissed Jesus, what did the men do to Him?

Memory Verse

Now faith is being sure of what we hope for and certain of what we do not see.

Hebrews 11:1

step 95

Taken Away

Matthew 26:47–56; Mark 14:43–52; Luke 22:47–53;
John 18:1–12

The disciples didn't want the soldiers to take Jesus away from the garden. A disciple named Peter took a sword, and cut off one soldier's ear. But Jesus told Peter to put his sword away. Then Jesus touched the man's ear, and made it well again.

Jesus did not want the disciples to fight. He said that God would send down many angels from heaven to fight for Him if He asked. But Jesus would not ask them to come. He was willing to let the men take Him. And He was willing to let them kill Him.

Why was Jesus willing to let the men do these things? Because that was the way He was going to be punished for all our sins.

The men took Jesus out of the garden. The disciples were afraid that they would be taken, so they ran away.

Questions

- How do you think the disciples felt when they saw the men taking Jesus away?

- What did the disciple named Peter do?

- What did Jesus do to the man's ear?

- Why was Jesus willing to let the men kill Him?

- When the disciples saw the men taking Jesus away, what did they do?

- What would you have done?

Memory Verse

Now faith is being sure of what we hope for and certain of what we do not see.

Hebrews 11:1

Death of a King

Matthew 26:57–68; 27:1–2,11–50

In our country, when people do wrong things, only judges can tell them what their punishment will be. But in Jesus' day, the governor could also punish people for doing wrong things. The men who wanted to kill Jesus took Him to the governor.

These men were very bad because they lied when they said Jesus had done wrong. Jesus had not done wrong. He claimed to be God's Son, which made the men mad. They said that Jesus was bad and should be killed.

The governor did not care about Jesus. He told his soldiers they could beat Jesus with a whip. It hurt Jesus and cut His skin. They got some thorny branches, wound them together into a crown, and pushed them down on Jesus' head. They spit on Him and called Him names.

Then the soldiers made Jesus carry the wooden cross through the crowds that had gathered to watch. They hammered great big nails through His hands and feet to hold Him to the cross.

It hurt Jesus very much, but He did all of that for you and me. He loves us that much.

The soldiers then raised the cross with Jesus nailed to it, and they stayed there to watch Him die.

Questions

- What did the men who wanted to kill Jesus tell the governor about Him?

- Were they lying?

- What did the governor do?

- What did the soldiers do?

- What did the soldiers nail Him to?

- Why did Jesus go through all of that?

Memory Verse

We wait for the blessed hope—the glorious appearing of our great God and Savior, Jesus Christ.

Titus 2:13

step 97

Jesus Is Alive!

Matthew 28:1–8; Mark 15:42–47; 16:1–7; Luke 23:53

There was a rich man named Joseph who loved Jesus. When Joseph saw that Jesus was dead, he went to the governor and asked if he could take Jesus down from the cross and bury Him. The governor said okay.

Joseph had Jesus taken down from the cross. Joseph wrapped up Jesus' dead body in some new, clean cloth. A good man named Nicodemus helped Joseph. They buried Jesus in a tomb that was hollowed out of a rock. Some women who loved Jesus saw where they buried Him.

The governor sent some soldiers to roll a big stone in front of the tomb, and then stand guard to keep Jesus' disciples away.

Early in the morning when it was still dark, God sent an angel from heaven. The angel's face was bright like lightning, and his clothes were as white as snow. When the soldiers saw the angel, they were so afraid that they fell to the ground. The could not move.

The same women had come back to look at Jesus' tomb. They wondered who would roll away the big stone for them. But when they got there, the stone was already rolled away, and an angel was there. The women were afraid. But the angel said, "Do not be afraid, for I know that you are looking for Jesus, who was crucified. He is not here; He has risen."

Jesus had told His disciples that He would be killed. He had also said that He would come back to life and leave the grave after He had been buried. Jesus did what He had said He would do!

Questions

- Where did Joseph and Nicodemus bury Jesus?
- Whom did the governor send to watch over the tomb?
- What did they roll over the door of the tomb?
- What did the women see when they arrived?
- What did the angel tell them?
- Had Jesus told the disciples that He would come to life again?

Memory Verse

We wait for the blessed hope—the glorious appearing of our great God and Savior, Jesus Christ.

Titus 2:13

step 98

Go and Tell Others

John 20:19–21; Matthew 28:18–19

After He came out of the grave, Jesus went to the disciples. They were in a room together. Even though the door of the room was closed, Jesus came into the room. The disciples were afraid when they saw Him. They didn't think it was Jesus; they thought He was dead.

Jesus told them not to be afraid. He showed them His scarred hands and side, so they would know it was Him. He had really come to life again.

Later, Jesus told the disciples, "Therefore go and make disciples of all nations, baptizing them in the name of the Father and of the Son and of the Holy Spirit, and teaching them to obey everything I have commanded you." He wanted everyone to know how much He loved them and that He had been punished in their place by dying on the cross for them. Jesus wanted the disciples to go all over the world to tell every person about Him.

Questions

- How did the disciples feel when they saw Jesus?

- Why were they afraid?

- What did Jesus show them so they would know He had really come to life again?

- What did He tell the disciples to do?

- What does He want you and me to do?

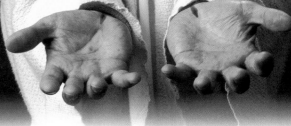

Memory Verse

We wait for the blessed hope—the glorious appearing of our great God and Savior, Jesus Christ.

Titus 2:13

step 99

In Heaven

Luke 24:50; Acts 1:9–10

After Jesus talked to the disciples, He took them out of the city to a place by themselves. While He was speaking to them, all of a sudden He began to go up into the sky. He went up higher and higher, until they saw Him go into a cloud. Soon they could not see Him anymore.

Two angels appeared and told the disciples, "Men of Galilee, why do you stand here looking into the sky? This same Jesus, who has been taken from you into heaven, will come back the same way you have seen him go to heaven."

Jesus is in heaven now. But He sees all of us as if He were here with us—and He is!

We don't ever need be afraid, for Jesus does not forget us. He hears us when we pray to Him, and He helps us to be good. When He comes to this world again, at the Second Coming, He will call us all to Him. He will take us to heaven, and we will live there with Him always.

Questions

- While Jesus was speaking to the disciples, where did He begin to go?

- Who came and spoke to the disciples?

- Where did the angels say that Jesus had gone?

- Where is He now?

- Does He see everyone?

- How long will His followers stay with Jesus in heaven?

Memory Verse

We wait for the blessed hope—the glorious appearing of our great God and Savior, Jesus Christ.

Titus 2:13

Jesus Promises the Holy Spirit

John 14:12–18, 26–27

"I tell you the truth, anyone who has faith in me will do what I have been doing. He will do even greater things than these, because I am going to the Father. And I will do whatever you ask in my name, so that the Son may bring glory to the Father. You may ask me for anything in my name, and I will do it.

"If you love me, you will obey what I command. And I will ask the Father, and he will give you another Counselor to be with you forever—the Spirit of truth. The world cannot accept him, because it neither sees him nor knows him. But you know him, for he lives with you and will be in you. I will not leave you as orphans; I will come to you.

"But the Counselor, the Holy Spirit, whom the Father will send in my name, will teach you all things and will remind you of everything I have said to you. Peace I leave with you; my peace I give you. I do not give to you as the world gives. Do not let your hearts be troubled and do not be afraid."

Questions

- When Jesus went back to heaven, who did He send?
- Where does the Holy Spirit live?
- How do we show that we love God?
- What does the Holy Spirit do?

Memory Verse

We wait for the blessed hope—the glorious appearing of our great God and Savior, Jesus Christ.

Titus 2:13

Life in New Testament Times

Many years ago there were trails that came into the land of Israel. They came from the east and from the north. Other trails came from Egypt in the south.

Traders used these trails to travel from one place to another. They traveled mostly by camel. They bought and sold goods along the way. The trails went *through* Israel. But they also *met* in Israel. It was almost as if Israel was the center of the world.

In a way, Israel *was* the center of the world. Jesus was born there. All of the things that happened in Bible times seemed to say, "Israel is a special land."

Places of Worship

The beautiful temple stood in the city of Jerusalem. It was the center of worship for the Jews. Herod built the temple again not long before Jesus was born. The temple was on a hill. Its shining white marble walls could be seen all over the city. Large stone gateways opened on all four sides. Jesus called this temple his Father's house (John 2:16).

Each Jewish town also had a smaller meeting place. These were called "synagogues." The leader of the synagogue studied the Old Testament and the Jewish laws. He then could teach the people.

On the inside synagogues looked much like some of our churches. The people sat on benches. The leader stood on a stage. A special box held the scrolls of the books of the Bible.

On the Sabbath day the people came to the synagogue to worship. The leader read a verse to call the people to worship. Then there were readings of thanksgiving and praise. Someone would lead in prayer. After that, the leader might ask someone to read from the Bible. Any member who was able to teach could give the sermon. The service was closed with a blessing.

The Laws of God

God gave the Jews the Ten Commandments and many other laws at Mount Sinai. Many Jews thought that trying to keep the law was the only way to please God. They began to add many of their own laws to God's laws. They began to see themselves as very good people.

Jesus told the Jews that they were going in the wrong direction. They were so busy doing many little things that they were forgetting the more important big things. They were forgetting to love others. They were forgetting to take care of the poor. They were forgetting to love God.

The Sabbath Day

God gave the people of Israel the Sabbath as a day of rest. On the seventh day of every week they rested from their work. They offered special sacrifices.

The scribes and Pharisees later added hundreds of laws about how people should keep the Sabbath holy. Then the people forgot that God gave the Sabbath to be a blessing. Instead they just worried about obeying all the rules.

On the Sabbath day people could not travel very far. They could not carry anything from one place to another. They were not supposed to spit on the ground. If they did they might be plowing a little row in the dirt. And that would be work! If a hen laid an egg on the Sabbath, they were not supposed to eat that egg. The hen had worked on the Sabbath to lay it.

When Jesus and his disciples picked some grain and ate it on the Sabbath, the Pharisees said they were working. When Jesus healed sick people on the Sabbath, the Pharisees got angry and wanted to kill him.

Religious Groups

The most important religious groups in New Testament times were the Pharisees and the Sadducees. The Sadducees were rich and powerful men. The high priest, the chief priests and rich businessmen all belonged to the Sadducees. The Sadducees were against any new group that tried to change Jewish life. That's why they were against Jesus and his disciples. The Sadducees also rejected many of the teachings of the Pharisees. They did not believe that people would live again. They did not believe in angels or demons. They did not keep all the laws of the Pharisees. They only kept the law of Moses.

The Pharisees added hundreds of laws to the law God gave Moses. They were mostly interested in keeping all these laws. But many of the Pharisees forgot some of God's other laws. They were proud of how good they were, and they did not love other people. However, there were also Pharisees who truly loved God and tried to do what was right.

Seventy of the most important Pharisees and Sadducees made up the Jewish high court. This court was called the Sanhedrin. The high priest led the court. The Romans let this court decide what to do when someone had broken a Jewish law. But this court did not have the power to put anyone to death. If the Sanhedrin thought someone deserved to die, they had to bring the person to the Roman courts.

The Roman Empire

Rome had begun to grow larger and stronger before Christ was born. Wars were fought and many new lands were added to the Roman Empire. This empire was very large. It included Spain and Germany, North Africa, Asia Minor, Syria and Israel.

Many good things happened because of Roman rule. There was peace between all of the different countries in the empire. The Romans also set up good government everywhere. They built roads for safe and easy travel. Many of the people were able to speak and understand the same language— Greek.

The Romans did not know that all these things would make it easier for the gospel to spread to many lands. They did not know that God had prepared the way for Jesus and the spread of the good news. Later Jesus' disciples traveled more easily to far-away lands because there was peace and because

there were good roads. They could bring the gospel in the Greek language to many people in many areas.

The Jews hated the Romans. They believed the Romans had no right to rule over them. They believed the Romans had no right to take their money for taxes. They didn't like the soldiers who lived in their country. The Jews also hated the Romans because they tried to change the Jewish way of life. The Romans wanted everyone to act like Romans. The Jews were looking for the Messiah. They thought he would become their king and would free them from the Romans.

The Jews hated tax collectors even more than the Romans. Many tax collectors were Jews who were working for Rome. Many tax collectors were dishonest. They took more money than they were supposed to take. They were cheating their own people to help the enemy.

Jesus often talked and ate with tax collectors. Matthew was a tax collector. So was Zacchaeus. Both became followers of Jesus.

Everyday Life

Life in New Testament times was much different from life today. It was a simple life. Most people did not have any extras. In fact, they often had just enough to live. The people worked hard, and children had to share the work.

Houses

The people built their houses of mud bricks that were hardened by laying them out in the sun. Sometimes the front part of the house had no roof over it. This part was like a small yard. Behind it was a living room with small bedrooms at the back. The floor of the house was of hard and smooth clay. Builders made the roof of heavy wooden beams with boards laid across them. They covered the boards with a mixture of mud and straw. This flat roof was a good place to work or sit. Sometimes

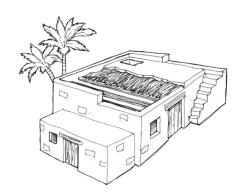

people slept on the roof on hot nights. Usually a ladder or sometimes steps led up to the roof.

Most people had very little furniture—just some wooden stools, a low wooden table and some sleeping mats. There was a place for fire and sometimes a small clay oven for baking bread. There was no chimney, so the smoke had to find its way out of the small high window openings. Some houses had wooden doors. Others had doorways covered with grass mats or cloth.

Food

The people ate foods like milk and cheese, grapes, figs, olives, honey and barley cakes, eggs, chickens, fish and goat meat, beans, cucumbers and onions.

The first meal of the day was usually bread and cheese. Sometimes a family would eat a light meal at noon. Again, bread was the main part. The people had their large meal of the day in the evening. They usually ate bread and fish, fruit and vegetables. The common people often ate meat only on very special days.

Clothing

The clothing of New Testament times was simple. Besides underclothing, the people wore robes with a belt tied around the waist. Over the robe they often wore a cape. Children usually had shorter, knee-length clothing. They sometimes wore a kind of pull-over shirt. Women decorated their clothing with brightly colored weaving and sewing.

The people wore sandals without socks. Their feet were often dusty from walking on their dirt streets and roads. They washed their feet often.

Work

The people did many different kinds of work. Some were farmers and builders and makers of pottery. Others were bakers and doctors and teachers. There were watchmen who guarded the cities. There were workers in leather and workers in metal. Jesus' father was a carpenter. He also knew about herding sheep. Peter, James and John were fishermen. Matthew was a tax collector. There were scribes who wrote letters and copied the laws and the books of the Bible.

Women had to work hard in their homes. The first thing they would do in the morning was make the bread for the day. They would grind the grain into flour, then make dough into loaves of bread and bake them. The women also had to carry water from the well and get wood for the fire. They made all the clothes for the family, spinning and weaving their own cloth out of flax and wool.

Parents expected their children to help with the work. Girls helped their mothers with all the household work. Boys helped their fathers in their work and were expected to follow the same trade as their fathers.

Schools

Parents taught their children Bible verses when they were still very young. They learned verses from the law and stories from the Old Testament.

When boys were five or six years old, they went to school. The leader of the synagogue taught them. For the first four years they studied mostly the first five books of the Bible. By then they knew the laws of God very well. They also learned how to read and write Hebrew. For the next several years they studied other books of the Bible and other Jewish writings.

When a Jewish boy reached the age of twelve or thirteen, he was considered to be a man. The boy and his family and friends celebrated with a special ceremony and often a party. Most boys left school at this age.

Conclusion

The time of the New Testament was the best possible time for Jesus to come. The people were looking for the Messiah. The safe roads made it much easier for early Christians to travel to spread the good news of the Savior. The common language made it much easier for them to tell others about Jesus. People were eager to hear about him. God had everything planned and ready.

Text for *Life in New Testament Times* © Zondervan.

Acknowledgments

Someone once said, "If you see a turtle on a fence post you know he didn't get there by himself." No book is the effort of one person. It takes a team! I am fortunate to have had an amazing team working together to develop the book you now hold.

I thank each one:

Catherine DeVries, Product Development Director, was the team leader and lead she did!

Sarah Drenth, National Accounts Manager for Sales, created a strategy for getting the word out about this book. You heard about it because of her work.

Kris Nelson, Creative Director, made this book beautiful and exciting with the creative design and myriad photographs and illustrations she doggedly hunted down.

Helen Schmitt, Associate Marketing Director. You hold this book in your hands as a direct response to her wonderful work getting the message out about it.

Kristen Tuinstra, Associate Editor, had to ride herd on me to get the book done. Her patience and her marvelous sense of humor were always an encouragement. She added her own creative writing talents to help me over the humps during my too busy schedule. All editors should be such fun to work with!

Wes Yoder, my literary agent and friend, who early on saw the vision for this timeless book.

And finally my children, their spouses, and my adorable grandchildren, who bring me such joy and pride as I watch them grow and mature in their understanding and application of God's Word to their daily lives.

Photography and Artwork Credits

Notes